GILARDI HOUSE

Barragán's Last Witness

José Luis Álvarez Tinajero | Martín Luque Pérez

node. + CASA GILARDI

Dedications and Acknowledgments
M.Arch, José Luis Alvarez Tinajero

For Don Martín Luque Valle (1948 – 2022)

Thank you for your affection, for your trust, for sharing your stories, for all the laughter, for your great sense of humor and your keen sarcasm... You depart full of the love and admiration of everyone who had the pleasure of knowing you. That is your legacy, farewell...

A very special thank you to Martín Luque Pérez Little brother, without you this project would not have been possible...

To the Luque family for allowing me to share their home with the public, not just the Gilardi House...

Very special appreciation goes to Alex Reyna. Thank you for your support and for believing in our project...

I am indebted to all the people who generously participated in this book:

Toyo Ito
Charles Renfro / **Diller Scofidio + Renfro**
Neil Denari / **NMDA**,
Ryue Nishizawa / **SANAA**,
Michelle Delk **/ Snøhetta**,
Paul Lewis / **LTL**,
Kengo Kuma **/ KKAA**,
Rafael Aranda – Carme Pigem –
Ramon Vilalta **/ RCR Arquitectes**,
Thom Faulders / **Faulders Studio**,
Alvin Huang / **SDA**,
Gerard Loozekoot / **UN Studio**,
Julio Jiménez Sarabia / **ULSA**,
Jorge Vázquez del Mercado / **UAS**,
Ricardo Devesa,
Antonio Cárabez Sandoval,
Leonora Flores,
Eduardo Luque Pérez,
César Béjar and
Carlos Alcocer.

I would like to express my gratitude to the people who contributed and made this book possible:

Alejandro Reyna, Gerardo Broissin / **Broissin Arquitectos**, Homero Hernández Tena / **ULSA**, Jorge Iturbe / **ULSA**, Mario Trejo Cuevas / **ACI**, Arq. Luis Méndez / **LUMEN**.

To you...

Margarita Tinajero Montoya, José Luis Álvarez Hernández, Gabriella, Yvette, Sebastián, Samantha, Peter, Pao, Ale, Emma, Marta García Martínez, Agus and Lucia Fortuna.

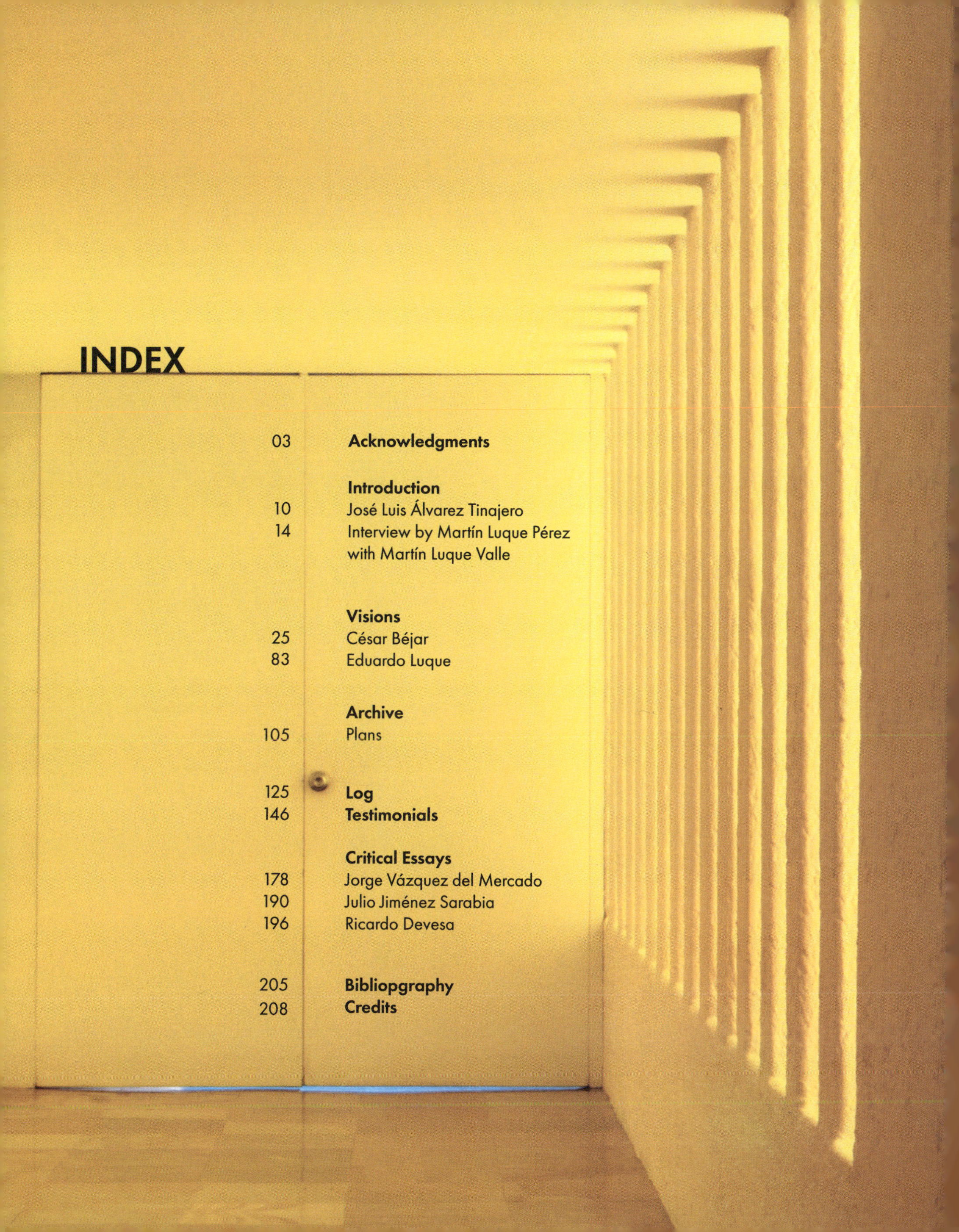

INDEX

03 **Acknowledgments**

Introduction
10 José Luis Álvarez Tinajero
14 Interview by Martín Luque Pérez with Martín Luque Valle

Visions
25 César Béjar
83 Eduardo Luque

Archive
105 Plans

125 **Log**
146 **Testimonials**

Critical Essays
178 Jorge Vázquez del Mercado
190 Julio Jiménez Sarabia
196 Ricardo Devesa

205 **Bibliopgraphy**
208 **Credits**

Introduction - José Luis Álvarez Tinajero

Interview - Martín Luque Pérez a Martín Luque Valle

A very special history

M.Arch, José Luis Álvarez Tinajero - **node.**

The Gilardi House has a very particular and unique history that few people know about. The setting is Mexico City, between the late 1960s and early 1970s. Imagine an advertising company run by two partners and, more importantly, two great friends: Pancho Gilardi and Martín Luque.

What was going on in Mexico at the time? In 1966, the Architect Pedro Ramírez Vázquez was appointed president of the organizing committee for the Olympic Games to be held in 1968. They would be the first Olympics to be held in Latin America. The architect had just one task: to use this international sporting event to situate Mexico in the global landscape, presenting an image of the country associated with innovation and the avant-garde.

Thus, in addition to organizing the games, Ramírez Vázquez decided to create several cultural and identity-related programs around them.

He put together a team of more than 250 people including writers, researchers and designers, and he developed an incredible design, communication, and marketing system with support from people like Mathías Goeritz, Oscar Urrutia, Abel Quezada, Luis Aveleyra, and Lance Wyman, among others. This talented group was given the task of generating a "new national identity" to show the world an image of modernity in the country.

It is important to recall that, at that time, Mexico was going through an unprecedented political crisis. The terrible incident of the student massacre in the Plaza de las Tres Culturas in Tlatelolco occurred two days before the opening ceremony of the Olympic Games, under the mandate of President Gustavo Díaz Ordaz (1964-1970).

After the Olympics, Lance Wyman undertook several other projects in Mexico, including collaborations with Barragán, Goeritz and Legorreta, and it was through these collaborations that Gilardi and Luque were first exposed to Barragán's work.

Martín Luque said in an interview that they were impressed by Barragán's architecture after shooting an advertising campaign at Cuadra San Cristóbal. In the early 1970s, Gilardi and Luque bought a piece of land in Colonia San Miguel Chapultepec, a block from where their advertising agency was located on calle General León. They understood the land as an investment, but they did not have a specific idea for a project. They could not have imagined what would happen to the lot, much less that Barragán would be involved in transforming their property.

At the time, the advertising agency was very successful, their economic situation was optimal, they had a large portfolio of clients, and both partners were used to dealing with people from the entertainment industry and public figures, in addition to attending and organizing social events, parties, receptions, etc.

During a dinner Giraldi held with the architects Juan Cortina del Valle and Aurelio Martínez, who were close friends of his, he asked Martínez to design a house for the land they had recently purchased... a "Barragán style" house.

Aurelio Martínez immediately refused, arguing that he was not interested in copying anyone, or doing anything "Barragán style". With a tinge of sarcasm, he suggested they should just ask Barragán himself to design their house.

The partners were taken aback; they were sure it would be impossible to ask Barragán directly for a design. They didn't have access to him; it was absurd to even think about it.

Obviously they were familiar with the architect's work. They were aware of his professional relevance, and they had seen his work published not only in Mexico but in other parts of the world, so that idea was almost unrealistic. However, Juan Cortina offered to get them an appointment with Barragán, since they were acquainted. And that was how the relationship began.

Barragán agreed to meet with them and invited them to his house and studio located on calle Gral. Francisco Ramirez. Over a good coffee, and following an extensive conversation, he asked them why they had sought him out to design their house, what had motivated them, what ideas they had and, above all, what their ambitions were. Despite all this, Barragán explained that he had retired from the profession, for the second time, 10 years earlier, and that his focus was currently on large-scale real estate developments and, therefore, he could not help them and unfortunately had to pass on their project[1].

In parallel, it is important to mention Emilio Ambasz, the Argentinian architect and Curator of Design at the MoMA in New York between 1969 and 1976, considered a precursor of the "Green Architecture" movement.

Ambasz, who was familiar with Barragán's work and had met him years earlier, and who was a leading figure in an important institution, the MoMA, decided to visit Mexico in 1974 with a very specific mission: to organize a monographic exhibition of Barragán's work at the MoMA and present a new position with regard to the architect, recognizing him as a point of reference in contemporary Mexican architecture.

Emilio Ambasz visited Barragán to present his proposal, which only had one condition: that it would include a new, previously unpublished design. Barragán gladly accepted the challenge; however, he didn't have a new design to put in the show. At that moment, he remembered the project for the young publicists that he had turned down.

That was how Barragán told Ambasz that he had received a proposal from two young men to build a completely new house. He explained that he didn't know how real the project would be, since he wasn't sure if the clients had the financial means to make it a reality. However, Barragán asked Ambasz to go along with him to meet with them. He was curious to visit the site, and he wanted to talk about the project with Gilardi and Luque – all with the intention of finding out whether there was a real possibility of carrying it through. Having said this, the architect spoke with Gilardi and Luque and arranged to meet at calle General León 82 to visit the site. The young men could not believe that Barragán had asked them to meet and that he was interested in their project.

1. Note to the reader.
The first time Barragán retired was in the early 1940s. Tired of clients, he decided to step away from the profession and shift into to real estate development: for example, Jardines del Pedregal (a 3.5 million square meter project). It is important to highlight that this was a very important project for his career since, in it, he explored, created, and developed the relationship between architecture and nature, the landscape and the land, which he so often pursued – the concept of designing based on the place.

They got organized and prepared, and when they arrived at the meeting, they asked Barragán about his ideas, his needs, and his expectations, with Ambasz as a witness.

A curious fact to note is that, at the center of the plot, now the central courtyard of the Gilardi House, Barragán saw a huge, majestic jacaranda. The tree was part of the living legacy of the Japanese immigrant Tatsugoro Matsumoto, a landscape architect who had worked on the imperial palace in Japan, and the person responsible for the fact that, today, the color of the jacarandas still announces the arrival of spring in Mexico City.

They say that, during that first meeting, Barragán, in the presence of Ambasz, told Gilardi and Luque: "Don't cut down the jacaranda because I'm going to design the house around that tree." That is how the history of the Gilardi House began, with a few words and a sketch done in situ that confirmed, in a very subtle way, that the architect would take on the project.

We could write pages and pages about the history of this house – which has continued into the present...

We know that Barragán did not give many lectures. He was never part of the academic world, and he wrote and spoke very little in public about his ideas on beauty, aesthetics and architecture. He never wanted to get involved in theoretical matters or academic stances to describe or justify his work. He explained clearly and conclusively that he was self-taught and that he gained the vast majority of his knowledge and ideas through travel, books, conversations with friends, and, most importantly, an intuitive sensitivity that was continually nourished by his experiences, the passage of time, and his passion for what he considered to be "beautiful." He said something similar in his acceptance speech for the Pritzker Prize, *"Beauty" is a difficult idea for me to define, but I think we all recognize it when we are in the presence of it...*

That is why we sometimes rely on other figures to help us understand Barragán. Ambasz, for example, describes Barragán's work as autobiographical, and in this fragment of a text by Elena Poniatowska, the architect himself explains why:

My roots are in Mexico. I am lucky to have lived in the countryside, in small towns, and to have experienced life in a rural setting. My best memories and my fondest dreams are from my childhood. My childhood in the countryside definitely left an impact on me. I believe, as Emilio Ambasz says, that what writers, painters, and artists in general do is always autobiographical. Unconsciously, the memories of my childhood resurface in my work; that's why I design troughs and watering holes for horses, and it's why I choose ochers and reds, the colors of the earth, the colors of blood [...][2]*:*

To conclude, I would like to share a quote from an interview with Barragán that sums up his work as an architect in the most eloquent, sincerest way and that, as I see it, perfectly describes the Gilardi House and its significance:

"I realize that the only thing i have ever known how to transmit is my emotion..."

Luis Barragán

---

2. Elena Poniatowska, *Todo México*, Mexico City: Editorial Diana, 1990, Volume 1, p. 29.

An Interview by Martín Luque Pérez with his father Martín Luque Valle

Martín Luque Pérez: We're going to talk with my father for a bit to learn about his life, his experiences, and to look at Luis Barragán's work in a warmer, more human way. Sometimes it can be very technical or abstract, but we have an opportunity to make it more dynamic.

Let me introduce you to my father. His name is Martín Luque Valle, and he was born in Guasave, Sinaloa. My father had the good fortune of being Luis Barragán's last client, and that makes him one of the few people today who can tell us about the architect.

So, let's get started. Who was Pancho Gilardi, dad?

Martín Luque Valle: Pancho Gilardi was a publicist and photographer whose achievements were wide reaching: a man who was always ahead of his time.

I met him at a dinner at Ricardo and Rosalinda's house. From the conversation we had that night, we became very good friends.

MLP: When did you become partners?

MLV: That happened later, when I started working at a record label. I was hired by Jorge Alberto Riancho and Pedro Armendáriz Jr., Pancho's advertising agency did the branding. That was the beginning of our friendship. I was about 21 or 22 years old, and Pancho was 25 or 26.

I coordinated with the artists for cover photographs and other promotional material. So I had direct contact with Pancho, and we built a very good relationship. Time passed, six years or so, and at one point there was an opportunity for me to work with him at the agency.

MLP: How long did you work together? What did you do together?

MLV: There's no end to what you can do when you work at it. We started with new clients: large accounts like Samsonite, Capitol, Televisa in the editorial section, among many others. Our success and potential for growth were such that we decided to move from the Roma neighborhood – our address was Colima 396 – to the San Miguel Chapultepec neighborhood.

We moved to General León 65, and it was Estela, a neighbor and friend, who discovered that a small house was for sale at number 82. She called us and we immediately went out to see her; we bought it the next day. The agency was at its peak then.

We bought the land without any particular idea in mind. At the time, Luis Barragán was an inspiration for us. We used colored walls in our projects, inspired by what he was doing, or we used places like the Prieto-López House or Cuadra San Cristóbal as locations for our campaigns. That's where the world collapses around you when you catch sight of such beauty. From the gate at the entrance to the path, the fountain, the stables and even the animals: the geese, the turkeys, the sheep. Everything there was like something from another world. Incredibly beautiful. Just so lovely.

MLP: So you saw his work in the Cuadra San Cristóbal and you were inspired by its architectural language...

MLV: Of course, it was an inspiration. The idea first came up during a meal. It was May 1st; I remember it well. We were having lunch with the architect Juan Cortina del Valle, Eduardo Uribe and Aurelio Martínez. The idea was that we wanted to build a house in the style of Luis Barragán. With a similar language, with colored walls and all that.

Pancho, who was a close and dear friend of Aurelio's, said to him "You should design the house." Aurelio immediately refused, saying "I don't do copies, or styles, or imitations of anyone." After some discussion Juan said, as a joke: "Why don't you just ask Luis Barragán?" Pancho had a way to contact him because his uncle, Julio Gilardi, was a very good friend of Barragán's; they had a relationship through horses, but that wasn't an option.

Juan Cortina, the architect, also had contact with Luis Barragán's studio, so he asked for an appointment, and we got one! Monday at 11 a.m. We went more out of curiosity than anything else, to meet him and see what would happen. At the time, Barragán was already a renowned figure, very admired. A meeting with him? Let's go see what happens!

So we arrived at the meeting. We found ourselves face to face with Barragán, and the first thing he says, very solemnly, is: "Listen boys, my apologies, but I'm surprised that young people like you would want me to build a house for you. So tell me about it. Where did this idea come from? Why?" So we started talking about our experiences.

It was a great conversation.

MLP: What was Barragán like when he was winning over a client? Years later you realize that he was seducing you all the time. What was that like?

MLV: You're right. They welcomed us, invited us to sit on a bench while we waited. Then they took us to the room that's next to the famous stairs. I kept my eyes peeled looking around everywhere to see what was happening. When we got to talking, he said: "Boys, forgive me. I'm sorry, but I've been retired for 10 years. So, no. I can't design your house."

We went back to the agency, excited to have met him even though he hadn't agreed to design the house. Delighted to have had coffee with him and for him to have welcomed us in such a dignified and friendly way. Our visit had been a novelty for him too!

After about three months, we were at the agency one morning. The phone rang, and the secretary answered. It was Barragán! He wanted to see the plot at that time of day because that was when he liked the light. "Let's go, let's go, let's go!" Pancho was jumping for joy; he was a very excitable person.

That was the first time we saw him out on the street.

MLP: Who was he with?

MLV: That was our surprise. He arrived with Emilio Ambasz, an Italian-Argentinian architect who lived in New York. He had already worked on projects in Mexico, and he knew Barragán.

MLP: Right. Emilio Ambasz is an Italian-Argentinian architect who oversaw some of the architecture exhibitions at the MoMA. He has also been involved in the Venice Biennale multiple times. He is a pioneer of green buildings and is known in the architecture world for being a great manager. What did Ambasz want from Barragán?

MLV: The MoMA had decided to do a monograph on Barragán, and he was acting as an advisor. They decided that Ambasz, who had met Barragán and who also spoke Spanish, would be the one to visit him. That's why they were together that day. They called us because everything Barragán had done had already been published, and our proposal was the only new thing he had. Emilio convinced him to call us about the project "to see whether they had found someone else to design their house."

The first thing he noticed when he saw the land was the jacaranda that now occupies the courtyard. "This was planted by Matsumoto, the florist of the Mexican bourgeoisie. Don't cut it down because I'm going to build the house around this tree."

MLP: But before that, had he informed you that he would design the house...?

MLV: No, but once he was in the courtyard he said, "Here, I'll give you what you need, what you want." Then and there, he started sketching and when he finished he gave it to Emilio. It was the sketch he needed from Barragán to publish the MoMA retrospective.

That was a Thursday, and the following Monday the machines were already outside.

MLP: OK. In terms of the seriousness of an architect like Luis Barragán, what can you tell us? What was it like dealing with Barragán in the design process, during the construction, with the payments?

MLV: So, construction started on a Saturday. Barragán had a platform laid out with the jacaranda right smack in the middle. The tree looked beautiful there. In one conversation he told us, very humbly, that we needed to let him bring to life what little he had left in his head.

For us, that was incredible. We'd had experiences with clients we had created campaigns for. They would say, "Put this in, take this out." It was really annoying, and Pancho would be livid whenever someone rejected a project. So of course our answer was, "You're the architect, you do what you think is best."

Every week we would be handing over money; there were a lot of payments each week for salaries, materials, and they worked very quickly! The architect told us, don't worry about my pay. We had made two payments to him, and that was it. He never charged us another cent.

MLP: How did you raise the money? Aside from the company's projects, which was part of it, of course. There's a funny story you always tell, about when Pancho grabbed a check from you...

MLV: Pancho would say, go talk to the client and don't come back without the money. Because we have to keep this project alive. So I'd visit the client, and I'd come back with a check. That's what Pancho was like; he'd send you on your way and you had to figure it out. Every time I went to get a check, I'd come back with it to pay for the work, payroll, materials, etc. Before the house, we used to take trips on the Concord, first class, luxury hotels, you name it.

MLP: That was over.

MLV: That was over, plus our expenses were rising. We were setting up a photomechanics workshop with a scanner, which was a novelty at the time. It was the first batch of machines arriving in Mexico. Pancho said it was like witchcraft.

Well, we were the pioneers in Mexico. Still at the advertising agency. We worked 24 hours a day!

And as for experience, we kept travelling. Not as often, but we needed to know what was going on in other parts of the world, like Italy or France. They were always ahead of the game.

MLP: It's funny because, as architects, we often forget what a hassle it is to manage money. We have our own troubles of course, but we often forget about the human element, the whole process that's involved. Paying for materials, making payroll, and then the architect decides from one day to the next that he doesn't want a certain wall anymore. How did you feel about that kind of behavior?

MLV: Pancho would say, "That's crazy, what's he going to knock down now?" He'd talk to the bricklayers. "Here comes the madman. He's going to knock everything down." But we always let him do what he wanted. He seemed so excited about it. Every morning at 11, he'd come to check on the construction.

When the house was almost finished we were looking at a purple wall, and he came in with his samples looking for the color. He handed me his cane and walked to the other end. He was looking for the color of the jacaranda. He wanted to compare it with the Pantone catalog to match it.

It was the color of the flower that cinched it for him, because he had even considered an orange color, but when he saw the jacaranda he said, "That's it!"

And one day, I don't remember exactly when, 1976 or 1977, Chucho Reyes Ferreira was being given the Prize for Arts and Pancho said to me, "Get ready, José is taking us to get dressed because they're giving the Prize for Arts to Chucho Reyes Ferreira and Barragán wants us to go with him, no, no, no..."

MLP: He was a solitary person.

MLV: Yes. And we arrived with Luis Barragán and Chucho Reyes. Chucho couldn't walk anymore, he was in his wheelchair.

The award ceremony was very exciting. It's a shame there aren't any pictures...

MLP: Or Instagram. You couldn't do a live.

MLV: There was nothing like that, but imagine everything we would have recorded.

MLP: All the selfies.

MLV: Exactly.

MLP: Hey Dad, here's a question I've never asked you. When was the first time you visited the site and you thought, "Damn it. What the hell is this?" Because it isn't easy to understand. It doesn't look like a house.

MLV: We never understood it.

MLP: Not even in the very beginning?

MLV: I never understood any of it. Everything smelled like cement, brick, paint. There were workers everywhere, moving up and down, and piles of materials. The boxes of tiles arrived, the wood arrived, the flooring arrived. We had no idea what was happening.

MLP: You always gave him free rein.

MLV: Always. He worked on this project with so much pleasure, with so much joy, as if he knew it was a farewell. It was the same with the furniture. The dining room set, the bedrooms, the table in the middle, some of which have been around the world, by the way. They've been taken all around.

MLP: What's your first image of the construction of the house? Which wall were they building, which part? Where did he start? From the back, from the front...

MLV: He started with the building. The pink volume. And when he brought in new things he'd always say that colors didn't scare him, in the least. You know what I mean?

MLP: That's the joke, right?

MLV: That's the joke. And the pink – well you've seen it now; all of Mexico is painted pink. But then when you look at the codices, you see that those colors date back to before the Spanish arrived in Mexico.

MLP: Was that when you began to realize that this was special, that it was unique? What did you and Pancho say about it? Did it feel like you were dreaming?

MLV: Absolutely, and it opened our eyes even more...

MLP: When did you realize that you were working with an architect who was unique?

MLV: We always knew who Barragán was. But seeing the plans in a magazine in Paris was a blast. The manager of the bookstore asked us why we were so interested in it: because we live in this house!

The woman couldn't believe it. That happened to us once in New York too, with the Rocke-feller's cultural attaché. They gave us such a wonderful welcome. And we still didn't realize half of what was happening, until one day someone from Bank of America from the United States came and wanted to take pictures to advertise the bank.

MLP: I mean, when you were young you knew that Barragán was a famous architect, but that was it.

MLV: Sure, we knew about El Pedregal de San Ángel and all that, but we didn't understand that this was on another level.

MLP: And that didn't scare you? I mean, why is this company here wanting to take pictures? Why is this person here wanting to see it?

MLV: We thought it was because of the colors. It wasn't until much later that we realized what we had on our hands. It has been a wonderful inheritance that we have enjoyed, and you, my children, well, all the more.

MLP: When did you move into the house? Was it finished or was it still under construction.

MLV: It was still under construction. I was renting a place in La Condesa, on Culiacán Street, and Pancho was living in Tecamachalco. We figured that we could save on rent as soon as there was a bedroom with a bathroom. We had to move from one room to another as they finished construction.

MLP: You lived in the house while they were finishing the construction?

MLV: That's right, in parts, exactly. And Gloria, who was the cook, moved around too. And it worked just fine.

MLP: When did you realize that the house was finished? When did you feel like the hou-se was yours?

MLV: When Barragán shut the door and didn't come back. He came back eventually, but with Armando Salas Portugal. He came to take pictures, and with filmmaker friends who came to shoot a movie.

MLP: About what?

MLV: A northern film. There was an actress from Sinaloa who was in it: Chayito Valdez y Alondra de Guasave.

MLP: And the first people who came to see the finished house, what did they say?

MLV: They never understood. That it was too square. "It isn't prettier than mine." That's what they would say. "My child could have designed this." Or that it needed more furniture. But one day Barragán was looking at the walls and he said, "Don't hang little flowerpots or put pictures on my walls. They don't need anything."

MLP: Listen dad, and who was the first person who came who made you say, Look who's here! or Why are they here?

MLV: The painter Roy Lichtenstein. People you'd heard of from museums, from their work. And so it began. Architects began to arrive.

MLP: Who was the first architect you remember coming?

MLV: Charles Correa, the Indian architect.

MLP: What did he say?

MLV: He wanted to put in some benches up here. That he'd do it for free, that he wouldn't charge us. I told him the design couldn't be altered.

MLP: What did Pancho say? What was the dynamic like between you?

MLV: Life isn't a straight line. Because of work I couldn't even come for lunch, which was the plan. I couldn't because I was stuck there.

We used the house for the agency. We did shoots there, events, presentations, and if we did the meetings somewhere else, we continued at the house afterwards. Gloria would have the pork quesadillas ready, made from blue corn and with a green sauce. Or she'd make her famous shrimp.

MLP: Speaking of the kitchen, there are so many stories about this house. What can you tell us about Barragán and the kitchen?

MLV: One day Gloria went into one of the rooms along the hallway, and she didn't know Barragán was there. "Hello, sir. How are you?" said the girl. "Listen, is there anything you need?" he asked her. "Yes. Now that you mention it, every time people open the doors in this house, they spoil my soufflé." So he took off the door and he put a little window in it so she could see who was on the other side, and he put a fastener on it so you couldn't push it open. It was 100% her territory from then on.

MLP: Barragán had understood very well.

MLV: When she told him what was going on, he said, "I'll fix it for you". Then when Pancho brought him back brownies from one of our trips he went crazy because he liked that kind of thing. So Gloria started making them. She made them every week, and he was just over the moon.

MLP: Hey dad. When did you start collecting art for the house? Tell us about the art.

MLV: I was always attuned to what was going on. We had good relationships with people who knew about Mexican art, and we realized that it would be valuable in a few years.

MLP: Like Toledo.

MLV: Exactly. I bought my first print by Toledo when I was 21 or 22 years old. That's when I started to like it.

MLP: There's a story about the house that is really interesting. The painter David Hockney came for an exhibition when you were doing the advertising for Tamayo. What happened with Barragán then? Did Hockney come here to the house?

MLV: Well, Barragán liked Hockney and while he was here at breakfast, he painted a picture for him. He did some drawings, with a dedication. We took them to Luis Barragán.

MLP: What is your favorite visit? I know they have all been special, but who was someone that made you say "I can't believe I met him, he came to my house, I talked to him..."

MLV: They've all been wonderful. All of them. Before people come, you may feel like they're larger than life. But when they come to your door they're just people, who feel amazement and have conversations. Barragán would welcome them, and everything was wonderful.

MLP: Have you enjoyed your house?

MLV: Of course! The parties we've had, and the ones you've had too. Afterwards, you look at the house and it's fine, absolutely fine. There would be layer of mud, of grime, and the next day it would be back to normal, like nothing had happened.

MLP: What do you think of the idea that Luis Barragán's work should be experienced like a museum or that it should be a museum?

MLV: It's a house that a family lives in; everyone has their space. Visitors can enjoy it, they can use the pool; and now the new generations are coming, who are going to turn life on its head.

MLP: Bruno.

MLV: Bruno, who is very important. Carlos, who has just become a father. Emiliano, a beautiful boy.

MLV: Plus you know, there have been many offers. They come with their briefcases and their checks wanting to buy it.

MLP: What do you tell them?

MLV: I tell them no. What can I buy with those checks? They say, you can buy a penthouse in Reforma, one in Miami, etc. And I say, why would I do that?

MLP: How could I find anything better?

MLV: What could be better? And the conversation is over. I have three sons. And with my sons there's no expectation of that. But I get to decide when. Or you might decide to sell it one day.

MLP: No, I doubt that.

MLV: No no. Definitely not.

MLP: There's something very interesting. There are people who think differently about the house, who, for one reason or another, say that this is Barragán's worst work, the least representative, a whim, theatrical architecture. What would you say to them?

MLV: Tadao Ando didn't say that.

MLP: What did Tadao Ando say?

MLV: That his best projects were Capuchinas and this house. Tadao was here for three days. They did a film. And people saw it in Japan on the cultural channel or in a feature in Casa magazine, with a circulation of 180,000 copies in Japan.

MLP: The entrance to the exhibition was a mockup of the gallery from the house.

MLV: Exactly. The carpenters and engineers came to take measurements centimeter by centimeter, and the exhibition was built on a third floor, there in Japan. They made a water mirror and lit it with artificial light. It was a huge success. There were trucks in Japan painted in these colors: red, blue and yellow, with the name "Barragán" written across the entire truck.

MLP: What do you think about the people who don't understand the scope of the house? How can they understand the house without living in it?

MLV: Right, you can't. There's nothing they can say. We'll just be here, surrounded by this calm. Like during the Covid-19 lockdown, people would say: What a fantastic place to spend the lockdown!

MLP: That's the importance of houses. Not of hiring an architect necessarily, but of thinking about our ways of living.

Speaking of the pandemic, what would you say to people? Would you invite people to come back after the lockdown?

MLV: Absolutely, because we've taken advantage of this time to get everything in perfect working order.

MLP: Why share your house? Why open your doors?

MLV: Listen, Martín, at first we didn't do it. but people kept coming from all over. I am so-and-so, I'm from Japan, I'm from Italy; it was increasingly more frequent. Talking with Catalina Corcuera, she said, Martín, you have to open the house. If you don't, they won't leave you alone.

MLP: Exactly. You learn to live with it, and that's what we did.

MLV: And every day there are new surprises.

MLP: Do you want to share all these ideas with people?

MLV: Absolutely. I think I've always been generous. I like sharing.

MLP: How have the people who have come to the house surprised you?

MLV: I used to open the door for people. But now I can't do that anymore because they did a video interview with me that was seen all over the world, and now people want to talk to me. Three hours talking!

Of course, there are stories like the one about Bono, who let out a singing scream when he saw the house. Patty Smith too, and so many other musicians, singers, actresses, actors. One day a painter came from Los Angeles, who wasn't interested in architecture but was interested in the tree. She took splinters from the jacaranda to make a piece.

There's so much to tell, Martín. Because so much has happened. There are people who burst into tears when they come inside, others who almost break down. So many emotions. I really like it when couples come in, and only one of them is interested in architecture, but in the end everyone leaves very happy, because it sparks their awareness. Sometimes more than the architects.

MLP: So there can be a lack of sensitivity, a lack of humanity. Sometimes.

MLV: We always need to have that humanity, and simplicity, which I think is the best thing. Being comfortable with yourself, tranquility and, of course, being kind. Receiving what they come to give you. There has been so much love, so much admiration, so many compliments. It has all been wonderful.

MLP: There are a lot of people who thank you for opening the doors.

Have politicians come to visit the house?

MLV: The son of former president Ernesto Zedillo, who is an architect. His security came two days before to check every corner. One of Carlos Slim's sons-in-law also came. Security is of the utmost importance. When they brought Cartier jewelry for photographs, the second they finished the shoot they went straight back to the van.

MLP: People ask if the construction was trial and error. Always. Barragán's work was always trial and error.

MLV: That's true. On the stairs there is a wall that wasn't supposed to be there, but when he climbed the stairs he felt like it was necessary. He had it built, he had it torn down. He walked up and down. It turns out that the wall blocks out the noise. You don't hear the planes going by every two minutes. You don't hear them in the library or in the bedrooms. Nothing, you don't hear them.

MLP: People ask if there are spaces you enjoy more than others. You can't enjoy them all the same.

MLV: No. I enjoy all the spaces, especially when I'm sitting with a book. I still surprise myself by finding new favorite spots. Recently, with Emiliano we had a new experience up there. We had never really made the most of it. And it was wonderful.

MLP: What's your favorite space and why?

MLV: It's the bedroom, my armchair and the dining room.

MLP: Which armchair, the one in the living room or in your bedroom?

MLV: In the bedroom because you can see the front and the back. You can see the treetops in Chapultepec and the jacaranda flowers. You can see everything.

MLP: We should remind you that it isn't a museum, it's a house. Architects don't make homes, we make houses. People make homes.

Visions - César Béjar

82

The Museum of Modern Art
New York

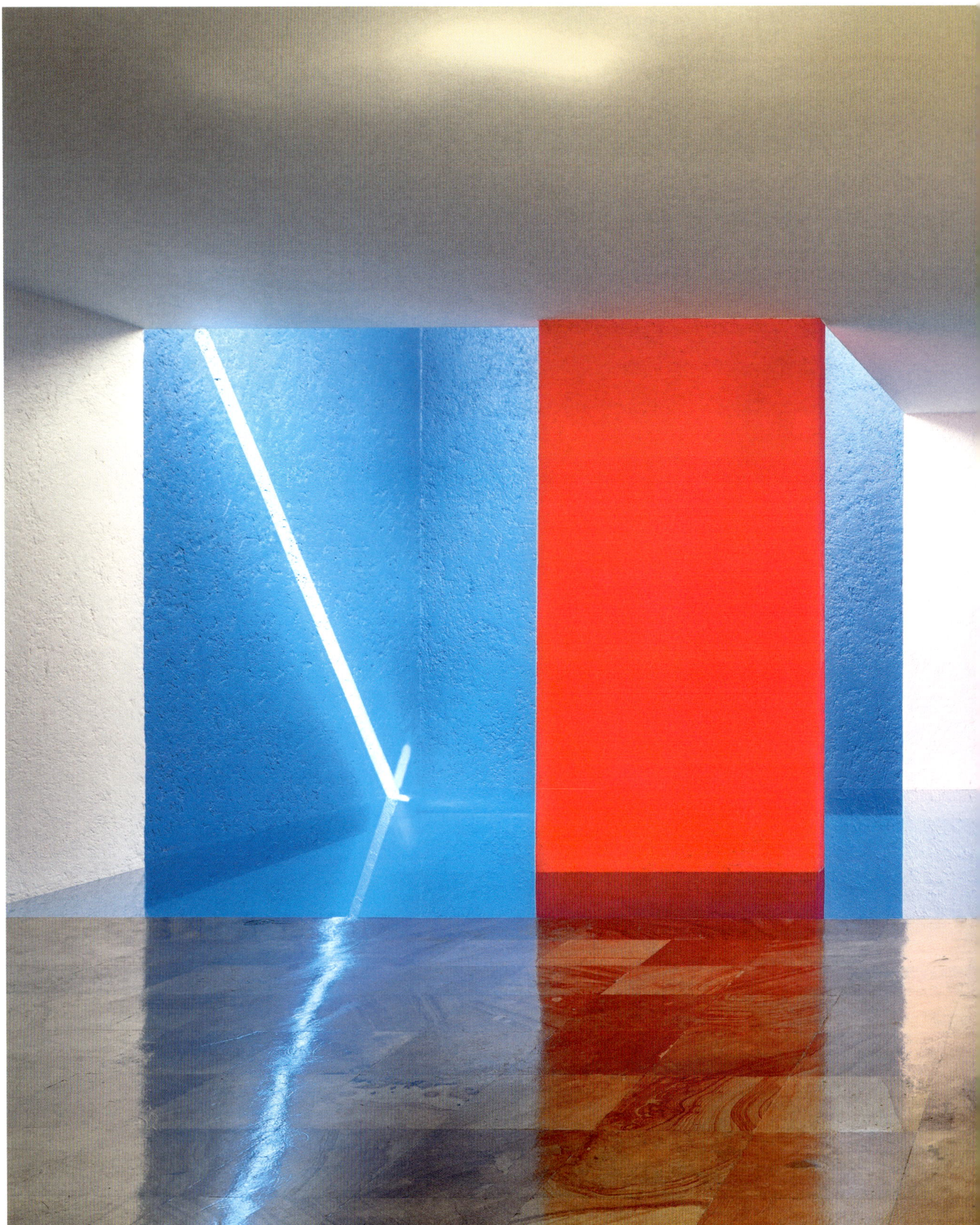

el Jimador
TEQUILA
RESERVADO
PARA
TODOS

PARA

BBVA

Visions - Eduardo Luque

Archive - Plans

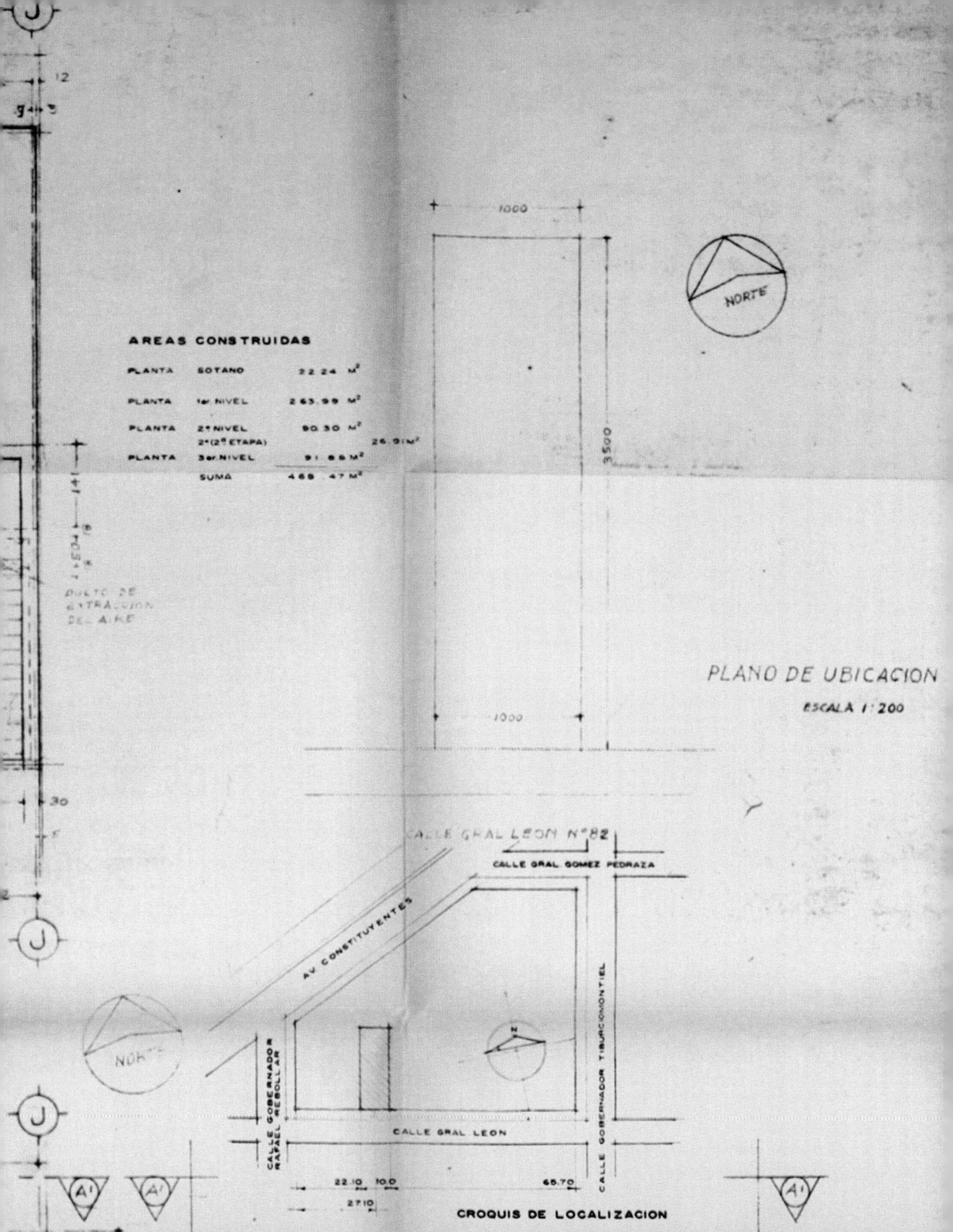

AREAS CONSTRUIDAS
PLANTA SOTANO 22.24 M²
PLANTA 1er.NIVEL 263.99 M²
PLANTA 2º NIVEL 90.30 M²
2º(2ª ETAPA) 26.91M²
PLANTA 3er.NIVEL 91.66 M²
SUMA 469.47 M²
1000
3500
1000
NORTE
DUCTO DE EXTRACCION DEL AIRE
PLANO DE UBICACION
ESCALA 1:200
CALLE GRAL LEON N°82
CALLE GRAL GOMEZ PEDRAZA
AV CONSTITUYENTES
CALLE GOBERNADOR RAFAEL REBOLLAR
CALLE GOBERNADOR TIBURCIO MONTIEL
CALLE GRAL LEON
22.10
10.0
65.70
27.10
CROQUIS DE LOCALIZACION

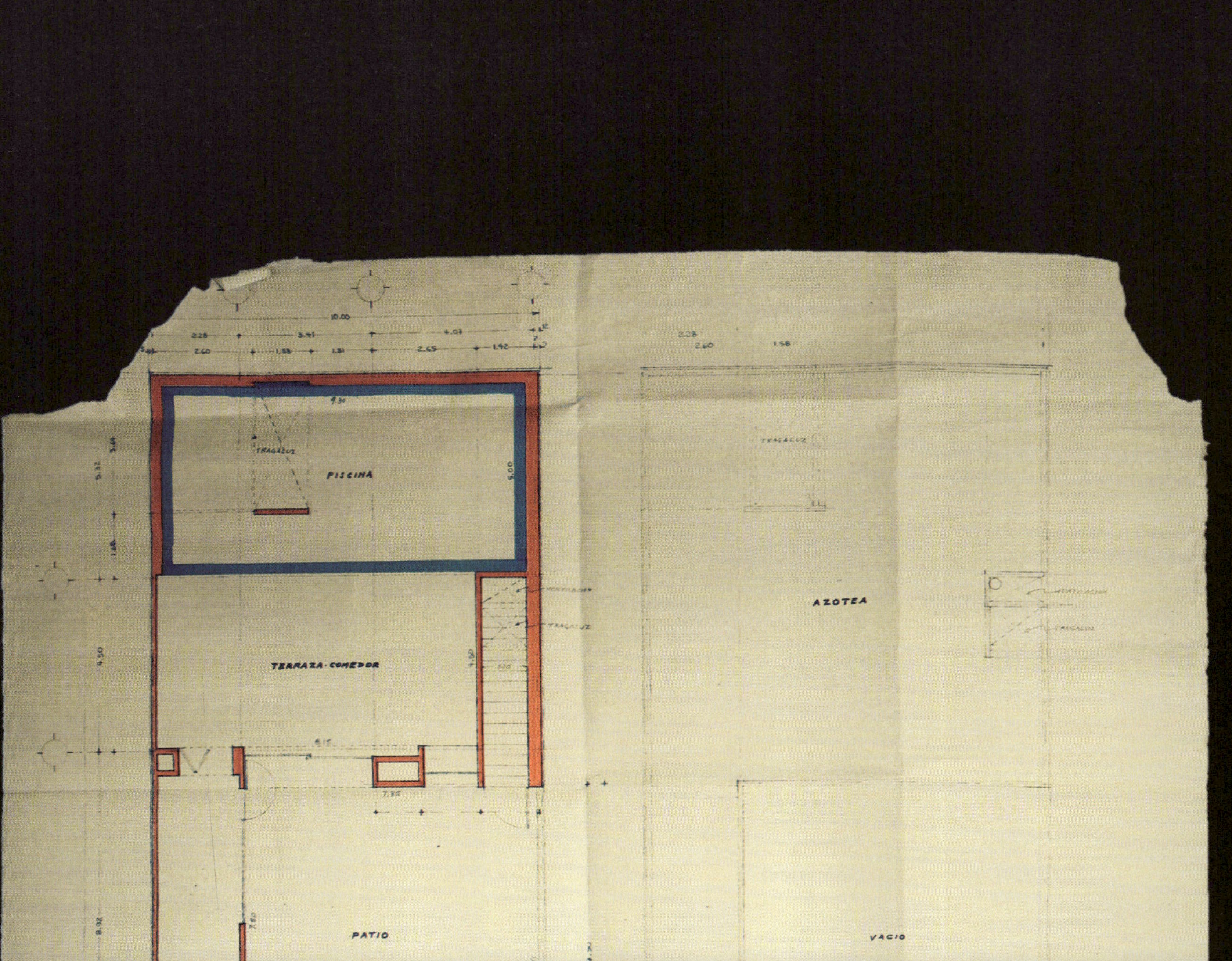

PISCINA
TRAGALUZ
TERRAZA-COMEDOR
PATIO
AZOTEA
TRAGALUZ
VACIO

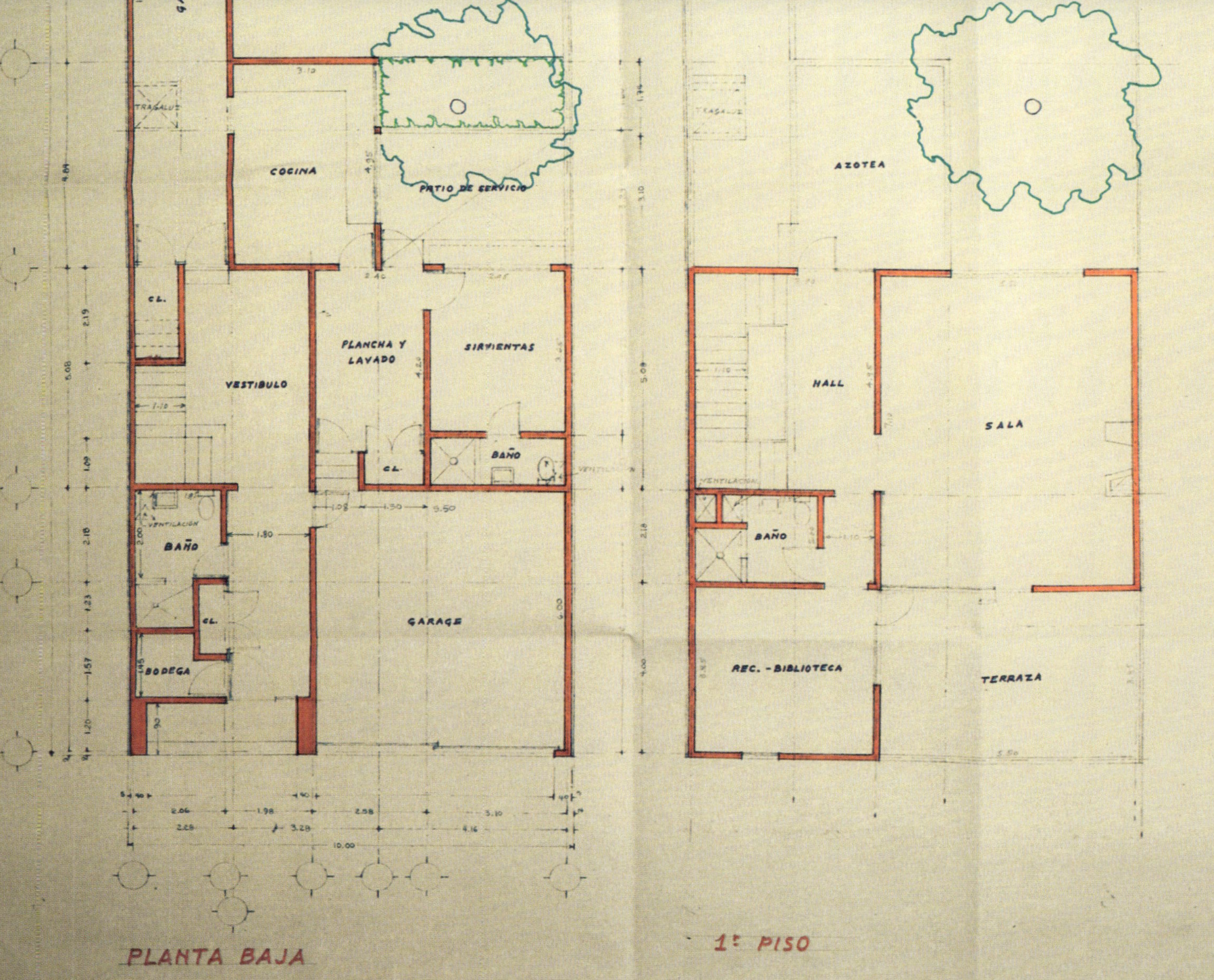
COCINA
PATIO DE SERVICIO
TRAGALUZ
CL.
VESTIBULO
PLANCHA Y LAVADO
SIRVIENTAS
CL.
BAÑO
VENTILACION
BAÑO
CL.
BODEGA
GARAGE
PLANTA BAJA
AZOTEA
TRAGALUZ
HALL
SALA
VENTILACION
BAÑO
REC. - BIBLIOTECA
TERRAZA
1º PISO
ESCALA 2 cm. = 1 MT.

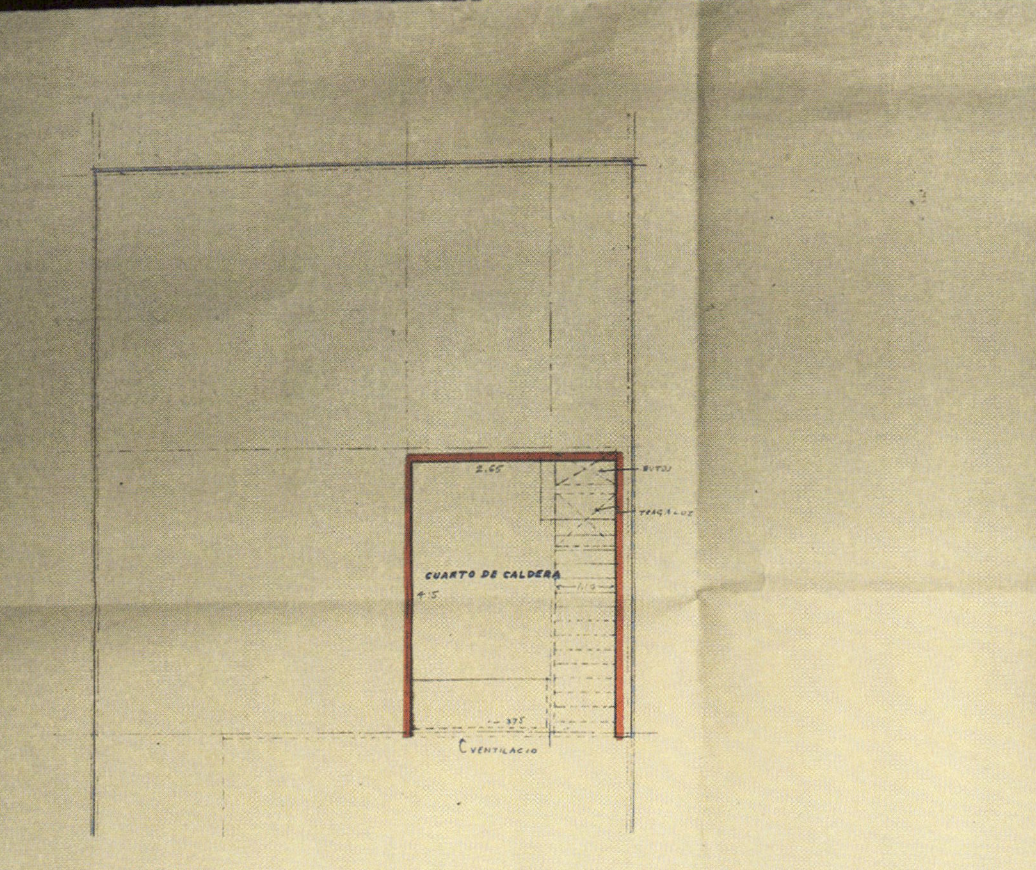
2.65
TRAGALUZ
CUARTO DE CALDERA
1.10
4.5
375
VENTILACIO
SOTANO

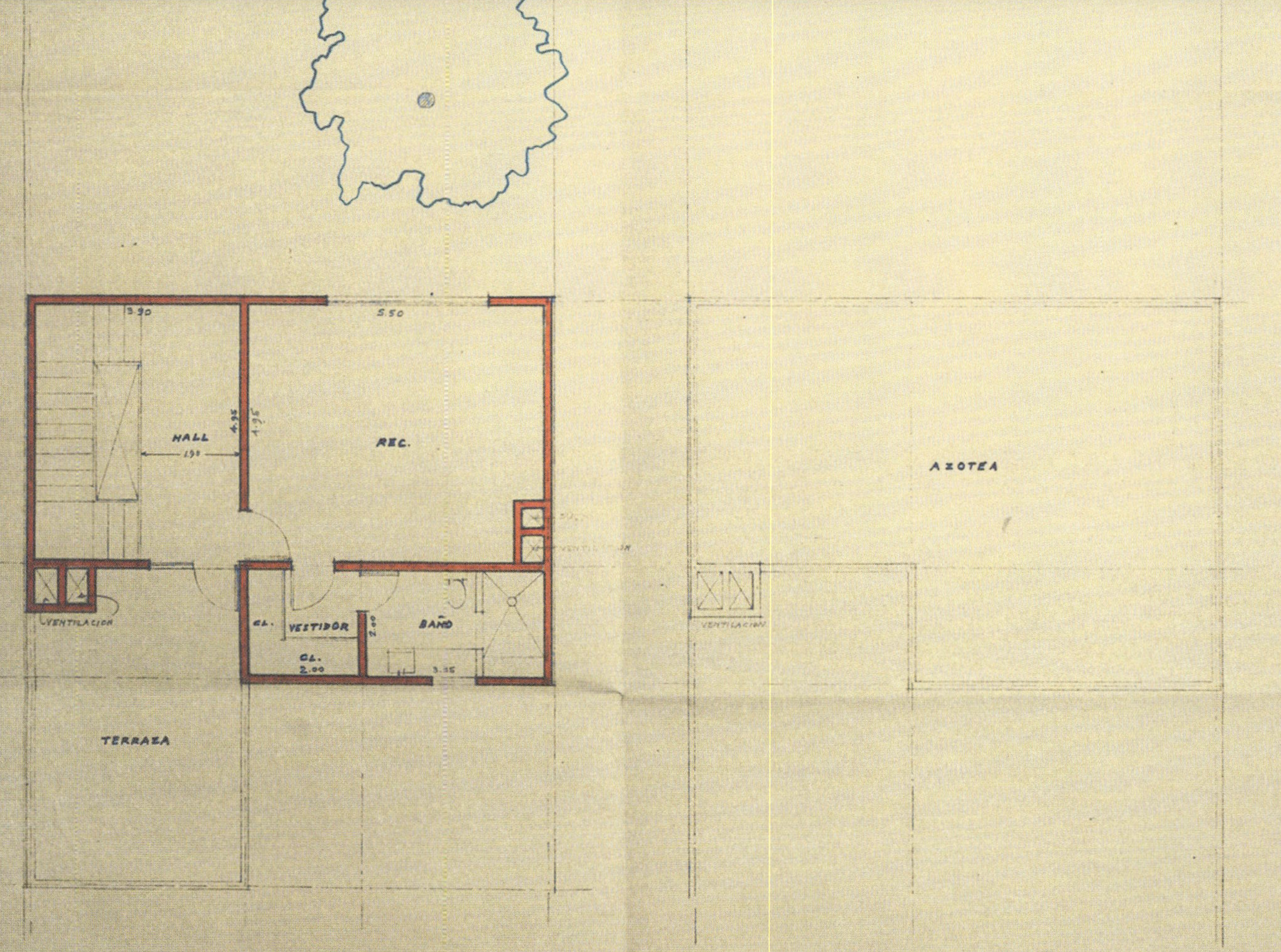

2º PISO

PLANTA AZOTEA

ESCALA 2 cm = 1 MT.

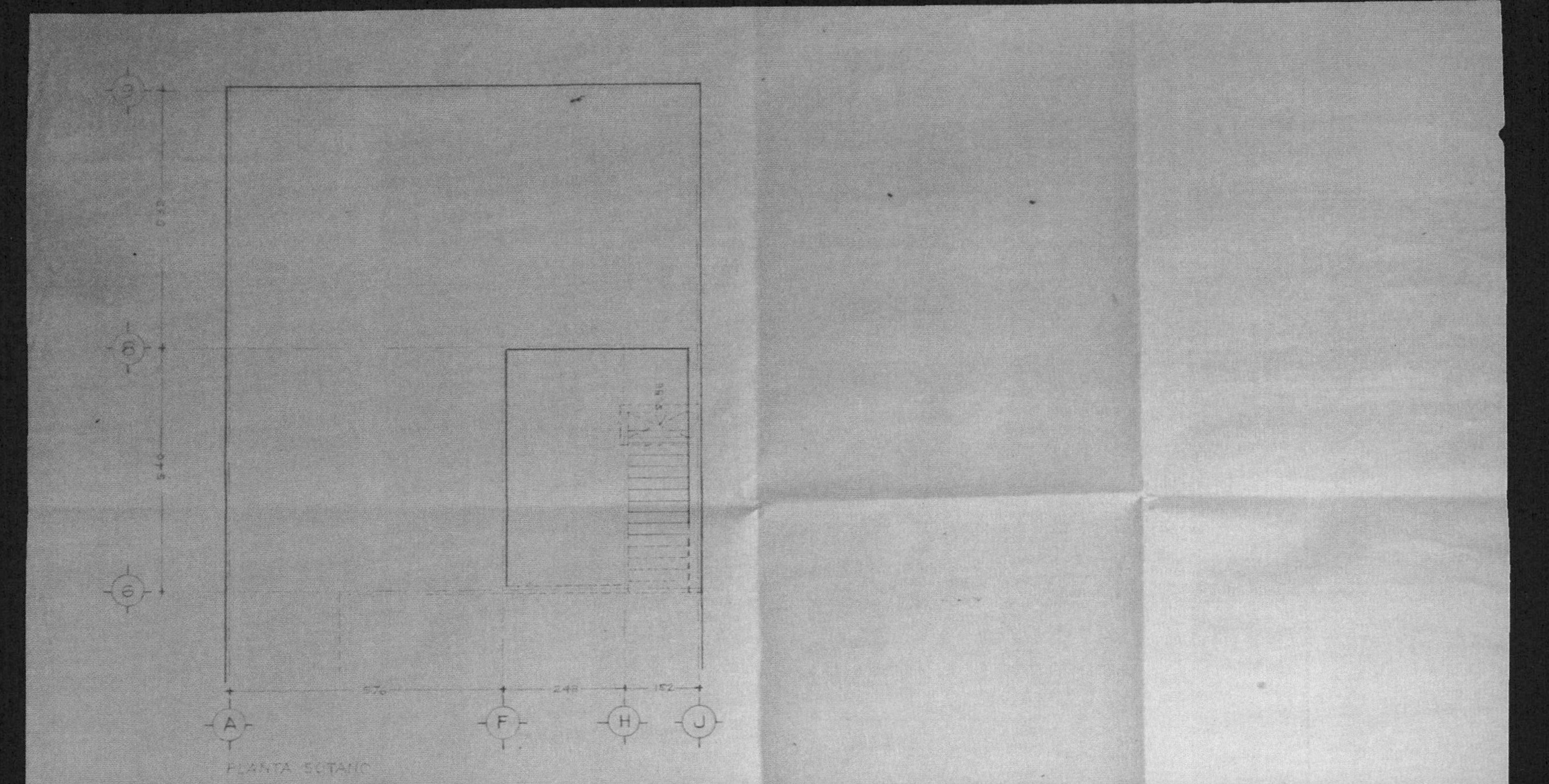

A
F
H
J
576
248
152
PLANTA SOTANO

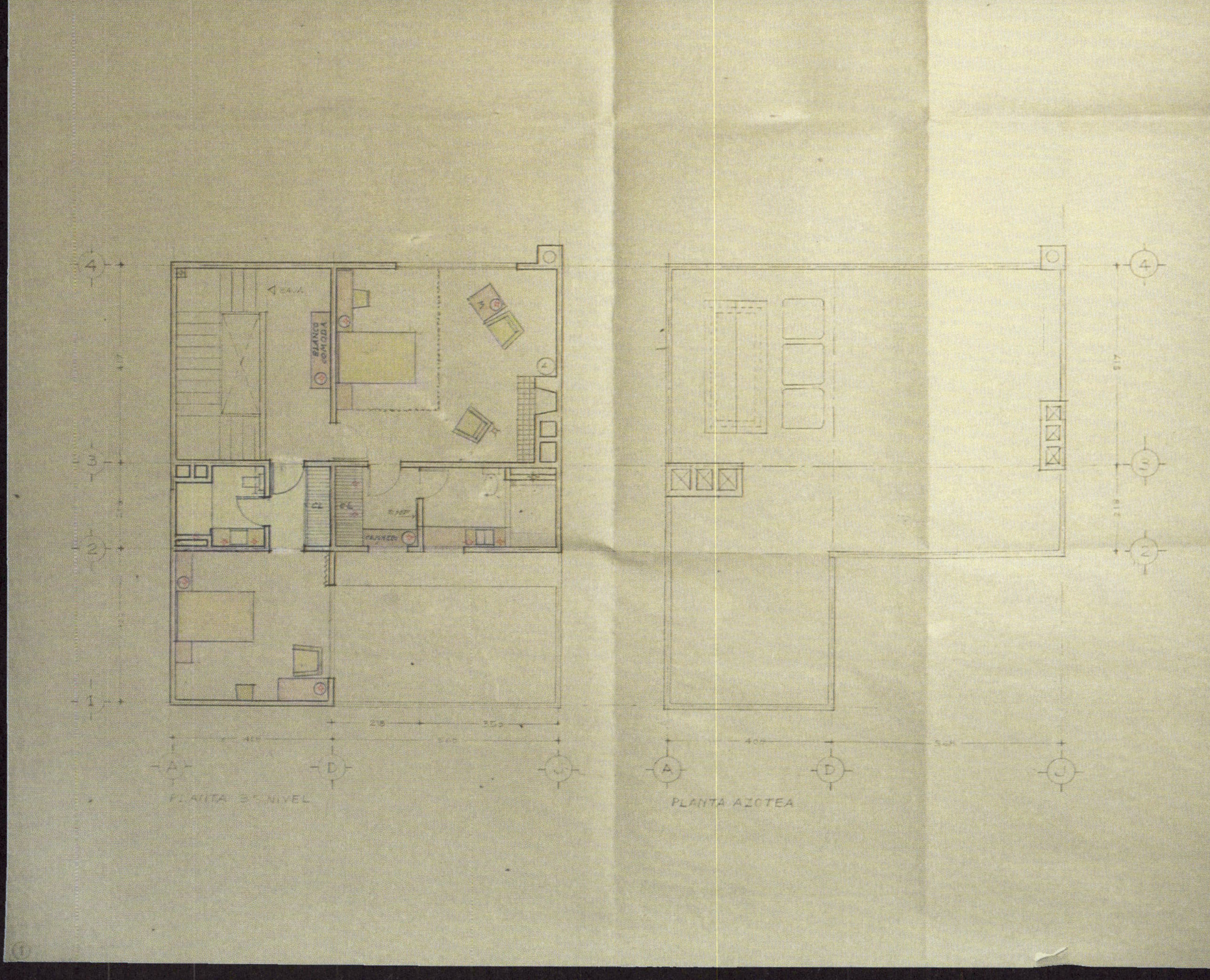

PLANTA 3° NIVEL
PLANTA AZOTEA

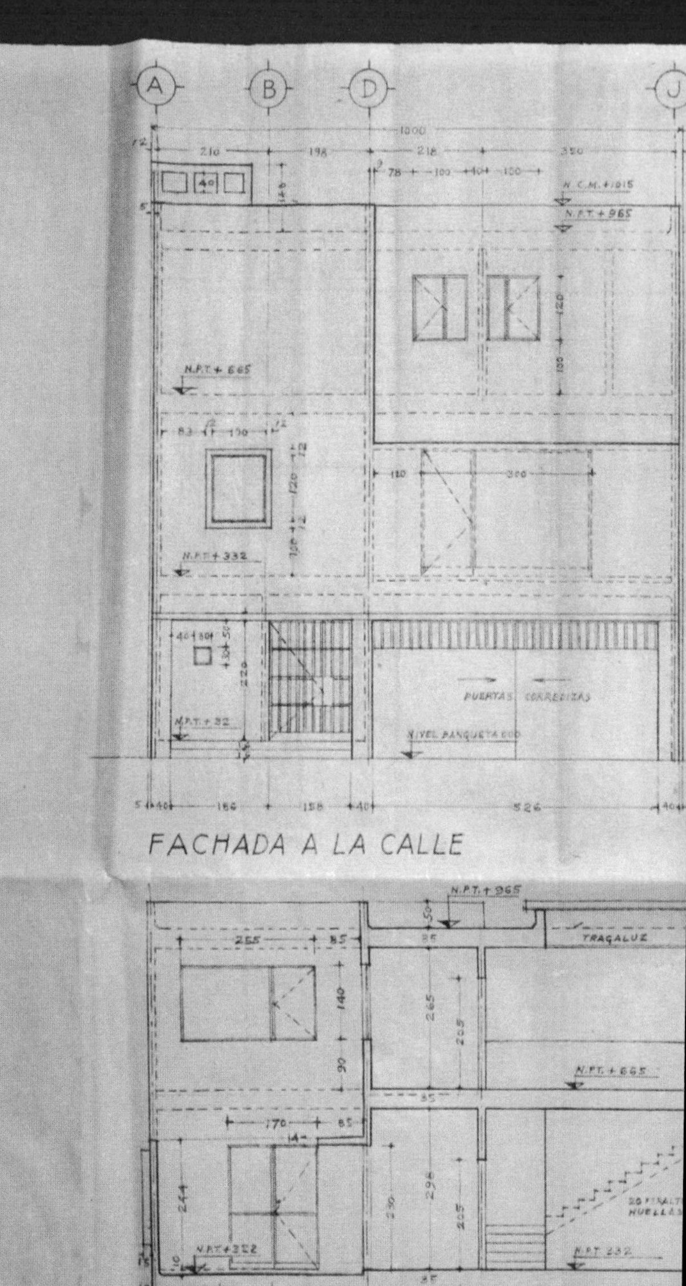

N.P.T. + 965

TRAGALUZ

N.P.T. + 665

N.P.T. + 232

N.P.T. 232

N.P.T. + 32

NIVEL BANQUETA 000

CORTE Y FACHADAS C'-C'

ESCALA 1:50 COTAS EN CENTIMETROS

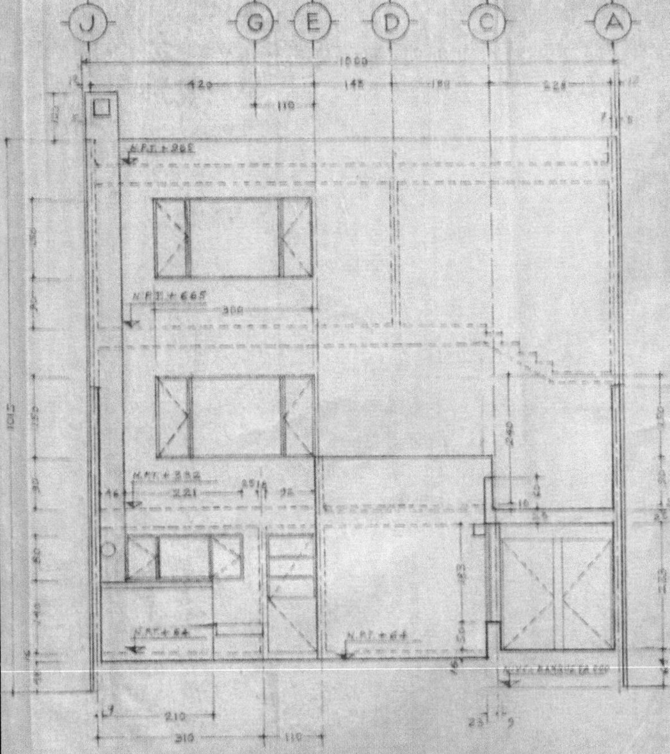

FACHADA NORTE A'-A'

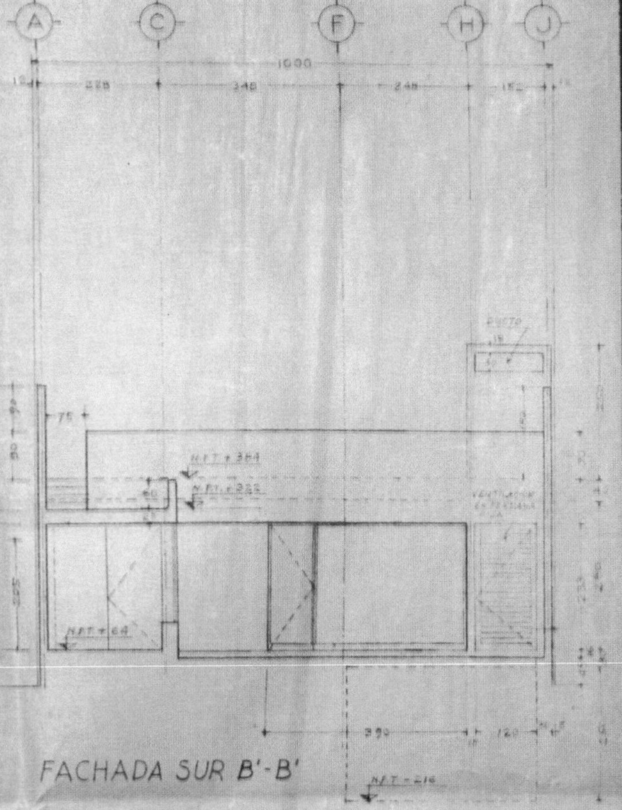

FACHADA SUR B'-B'

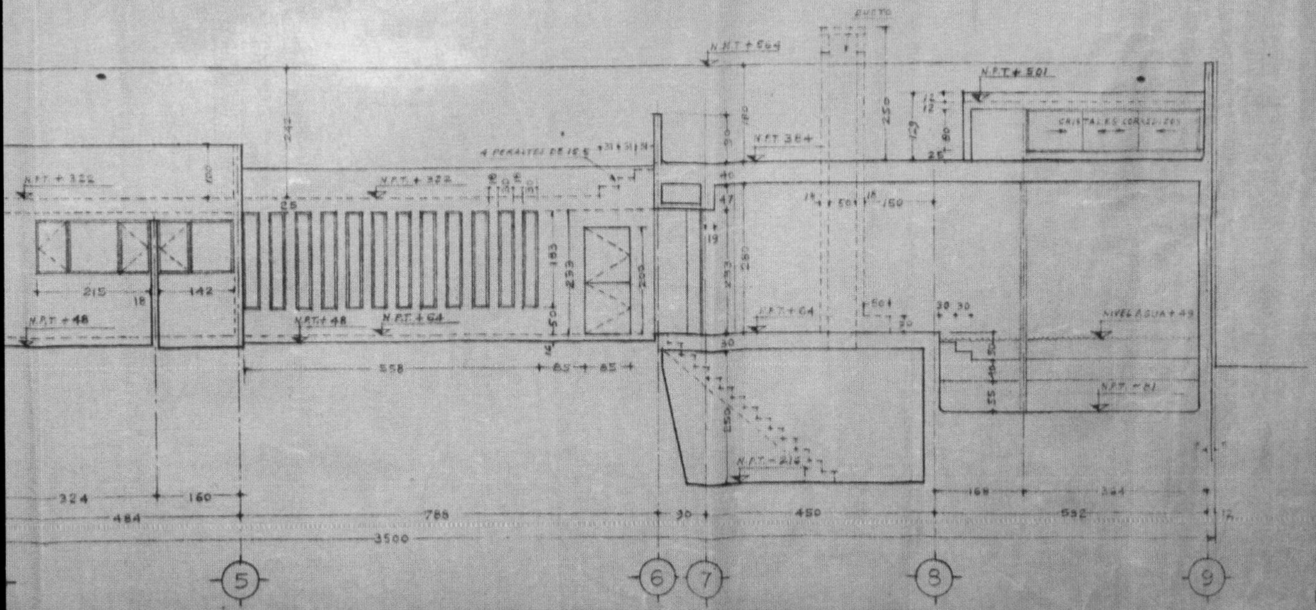

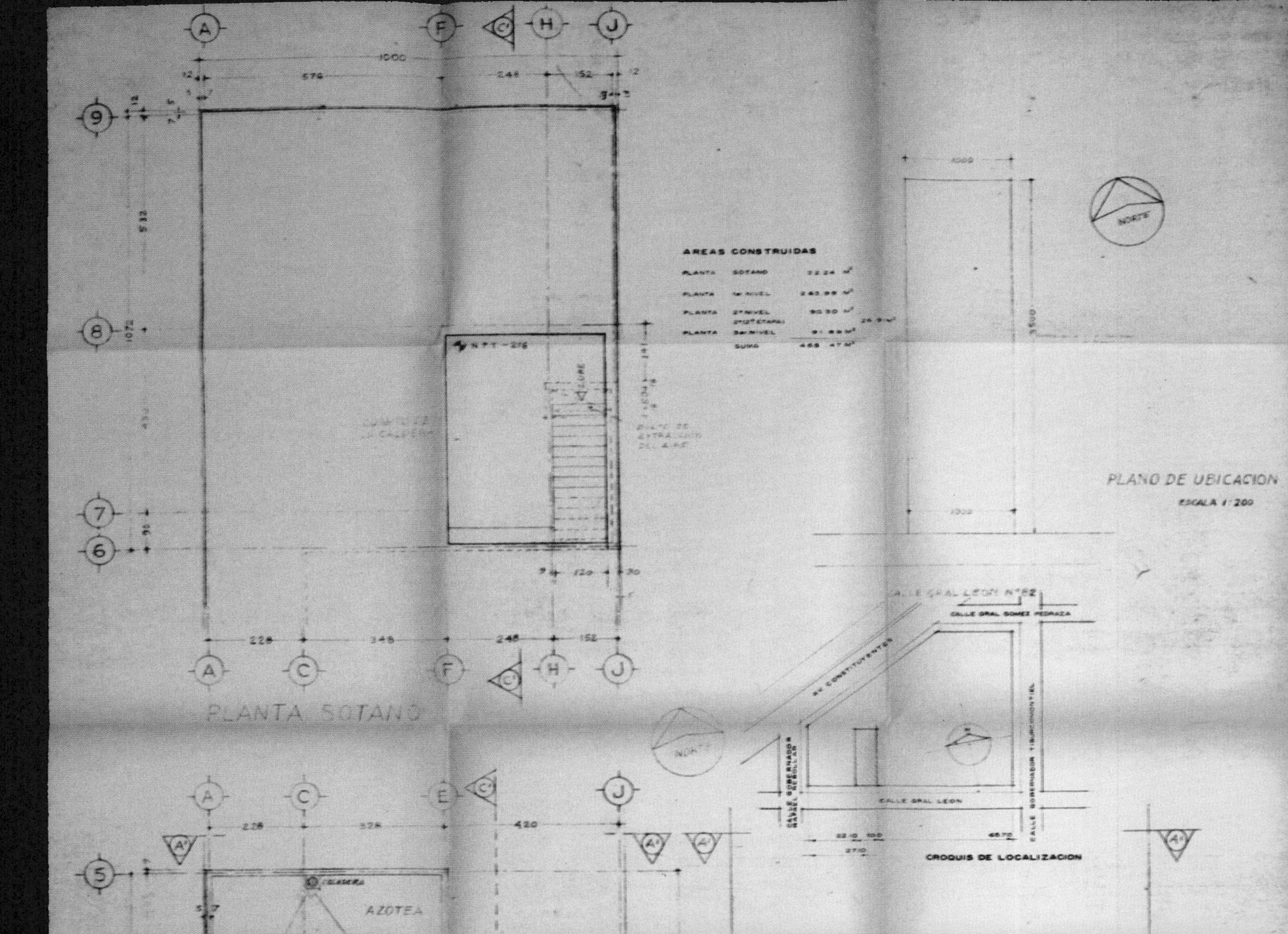
AREAS CONSTRUIDAS
PLANTA SOTANO
PLANTA SOTANO
PLANO DE UBICACION
ESCALA 1:200
NORTE
CALLE GRAL LEON Nº82
CALLE GRAL GOMEZ PEDRAZA
AV CONSTITUYENTES
CALLE GRAL LEON
CALLE GOBERNADOR RAFAEL REBOLLAR
CALLE GOBERNADOR TIBURCIO MONTIEL
CROQUIS DE LOCALIZACION
AZOTEA

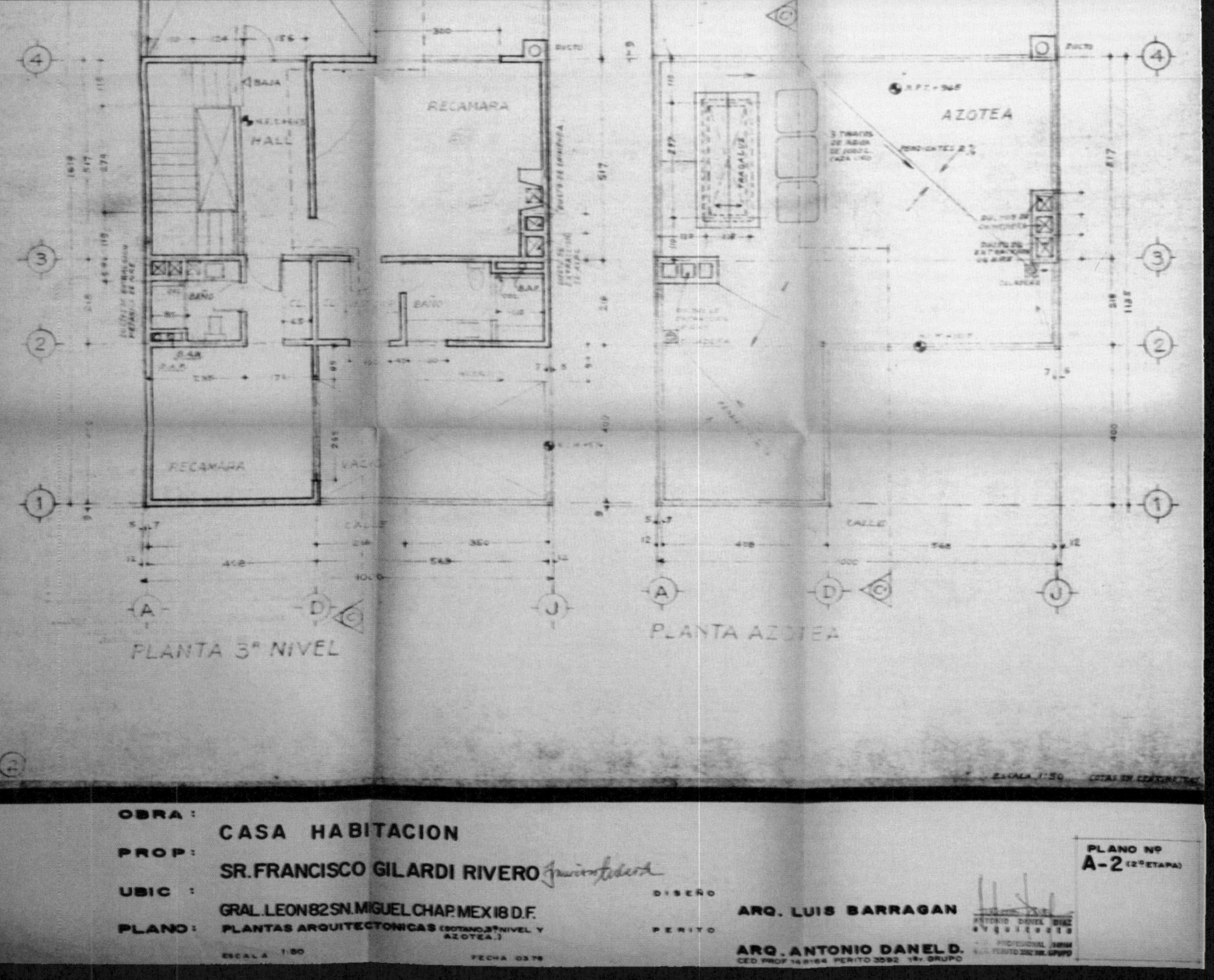

RECAMARA
HALL
BAJA
BAÑO
CL
RECAMARA
BAÑO
VACIO
CALLE
PLANTA 3ª NIVEL
AZOTEA
TRAGALUZ
PENDIENTES 2%
CALLE
PLANTA AZOTEA
ESCALA 1:50
COTAS EN CENTIMETROS
OBRA : CASA HABITACION
PROP : SR. FRANCISCO GILARDI RIVERO
UBIC : GRAL. LEON 82 SN. MIGUEL CHAP. MEX 18 D.F.
PLANO : PLANTAS ARQUITECTONICAS (SOTANO, 3ª NIVEL Y AZOTEA.)
ESCALA 1:50
FECHA 03.76
DISEÑO
ARQ. LUIS BARRAGAN
PERITO
ARQ. ANTONIO DANEL D.
CED. PROF. 14.8164 PERITO 3592 1er. GRUPO
PLANO Nº
A-2 (2º ETAPA)

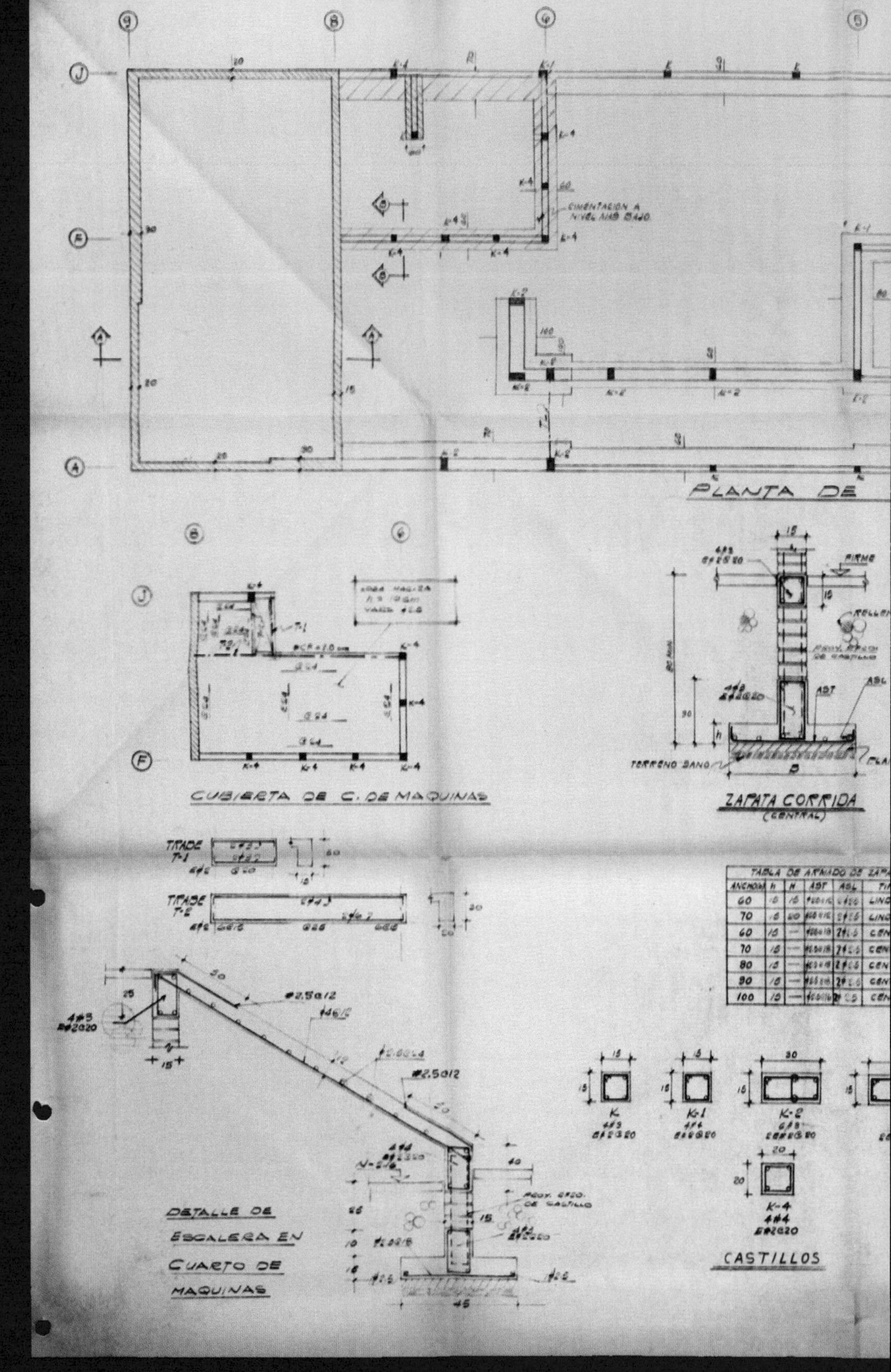

PLANTA DE
CUBIERTA DE C. DE MAQUINAS
ZAPATA CORRIDA
(CENTRAL)
TABLA DE ARMADO DE ZAPA
DETALLE DE
ESCALERA EN
CUARTO DE
MAQUINAS
CASTILLOS

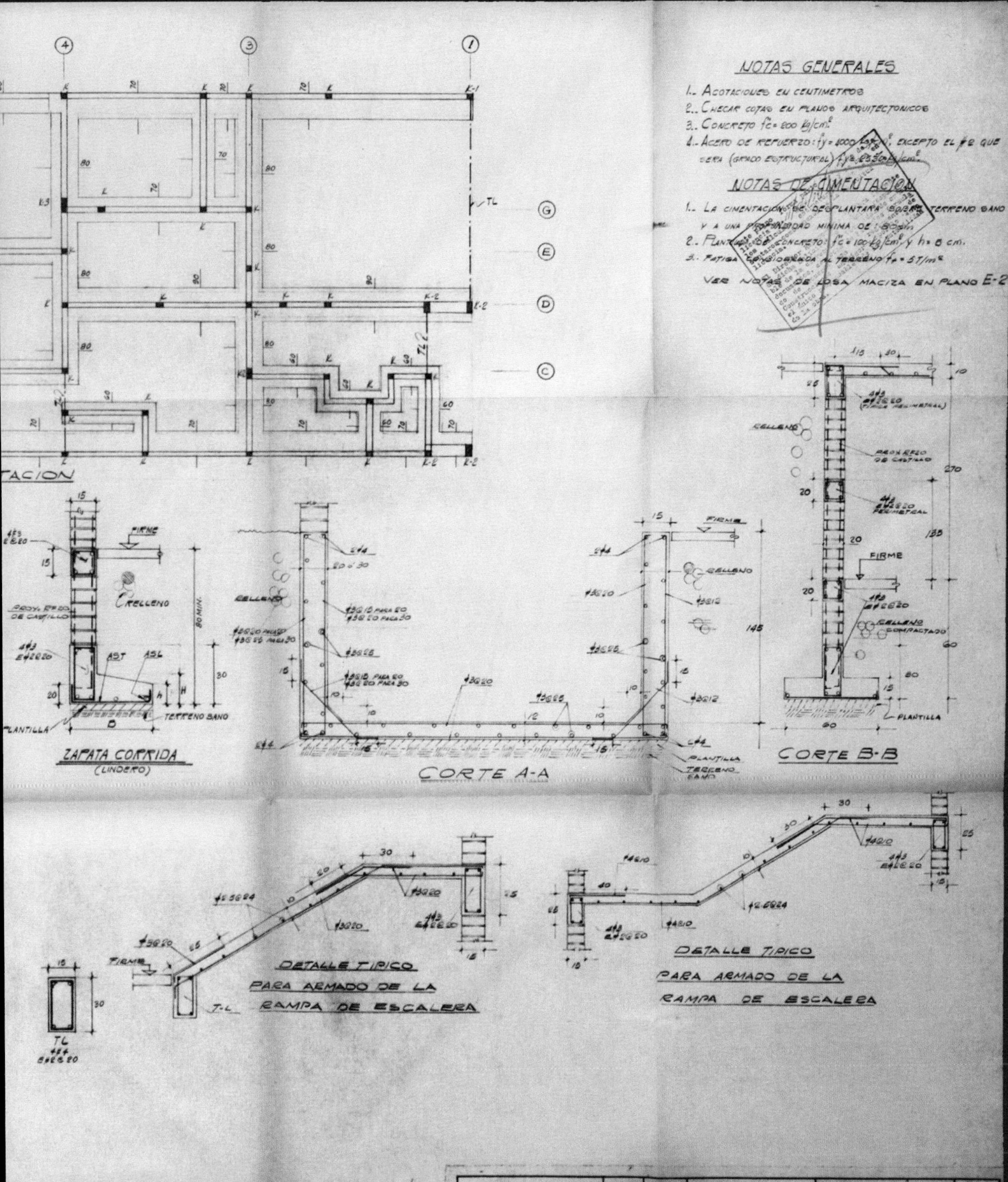

NOTAS GENERALES
1.- ACOTACIONES EN CENTIMETROS
2.- CHECAR COTAS EN PLANOS ARQUITECTONICOS
3.- CONCRETO f'c = 200 kg/cm²
4.- ACERO DE REFUERZO: fy = 4000 kg/cm², EXCEPTO EL #2 QUE SERA (GRADO ESTRUCTURAL) fy = 2530 kg/cm²
NOTAS DE CIMENTACION
1.- LA CIMENTACION SE DESPLANTARA SOBRE TERRENO SANO Y A UNA PROFUNDIDAD MINIMA DE 80 cm
2.- PLANTILLA DE CONCRETO: f'c = 100 kg/cm² y h = 8 cm.
3.- FATIGA CONSIDERADA AL TERRENO ft = 5 T/m²
VER NOTAS DE LOSA MACIZA EN PLANO E-2
ZAPATA CORRIDA
(LINDERO)
CORTE A-A
CORTE B-B
RELLENO
FIRME
PLANTILLA
TERRENO SANO
DETALLE TIPICO PARA ARMADO DE LA RAMPA DE ESCALERA
DETALLE TIPICO PARA ARMADO DE LA RAMPA DE ESCALERA
TL
CALCULO R. S. F.
DIBUJO A. P. C.
REVISO E. B. M.
FECHA ABRIL/76
INGENIEROS DISEÑO INTEGRAL
QUINTANA ROO No. 161 - 403 Z. P. - 11
5-74-40-29 - 5-64-74-31
PROYECTO: LUIS BARRAGAN arquitecto.
PROPIETARIO: SR. FRANCISCO GILARDI RIVERO.
GENERAL LEON No. 82
UBIC. MEXICO 18, D. F.
CIMENTACION.
PLANO E-1
ANTONIO DANEL DIAZ arquitecto

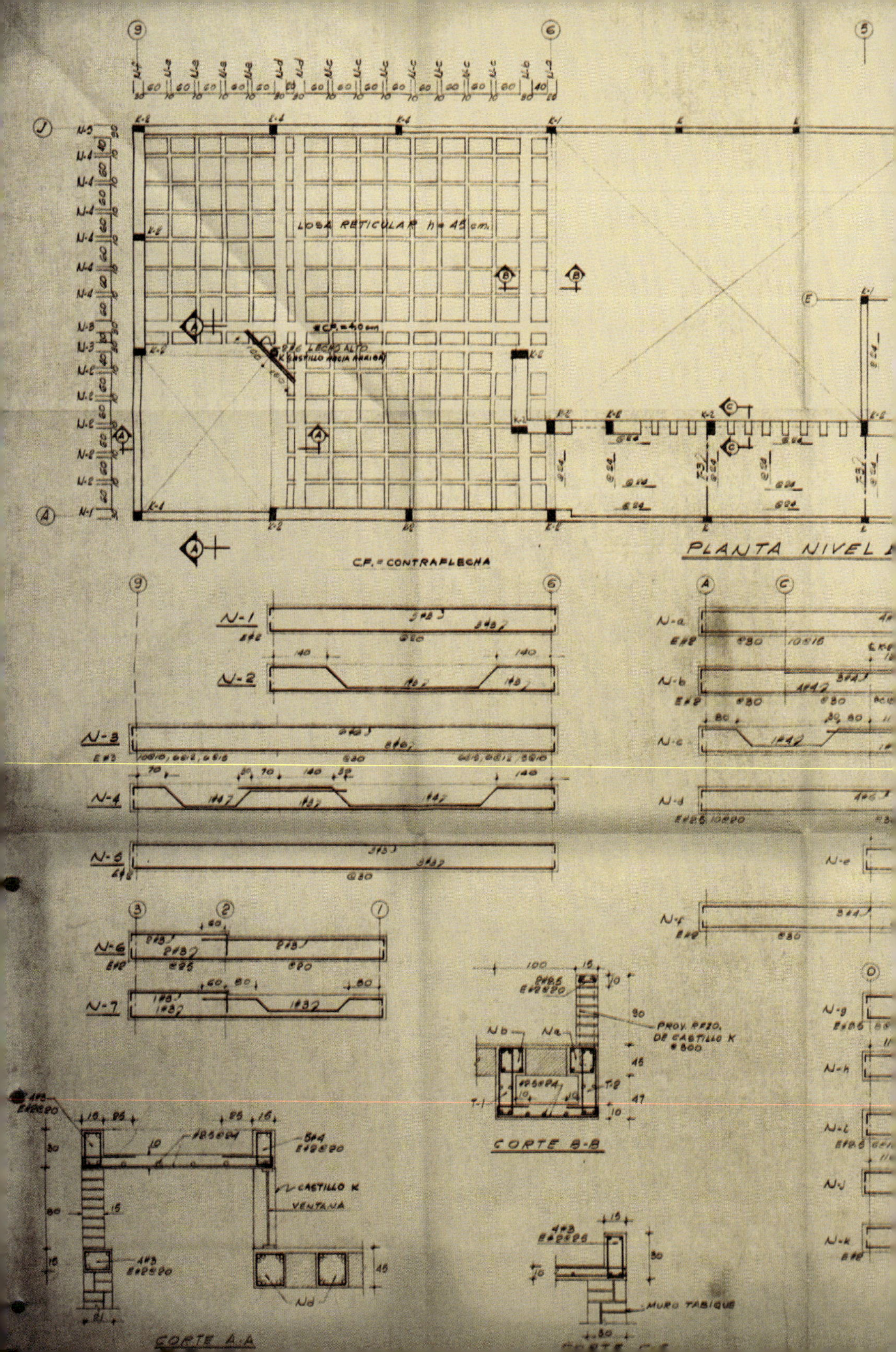

LOSA RETICULAR h = 45 cm.
C.F. = CONTRAFLECHA
PLANTA NIVEL
N-1
N-2
N-3
N-4
N-5
N-6
N-7
PROY. PF20. DE CASTILLO K
CORTE B-B
CASTILLO K
VENTANA
CORTE A-A
MURO TABIQUE

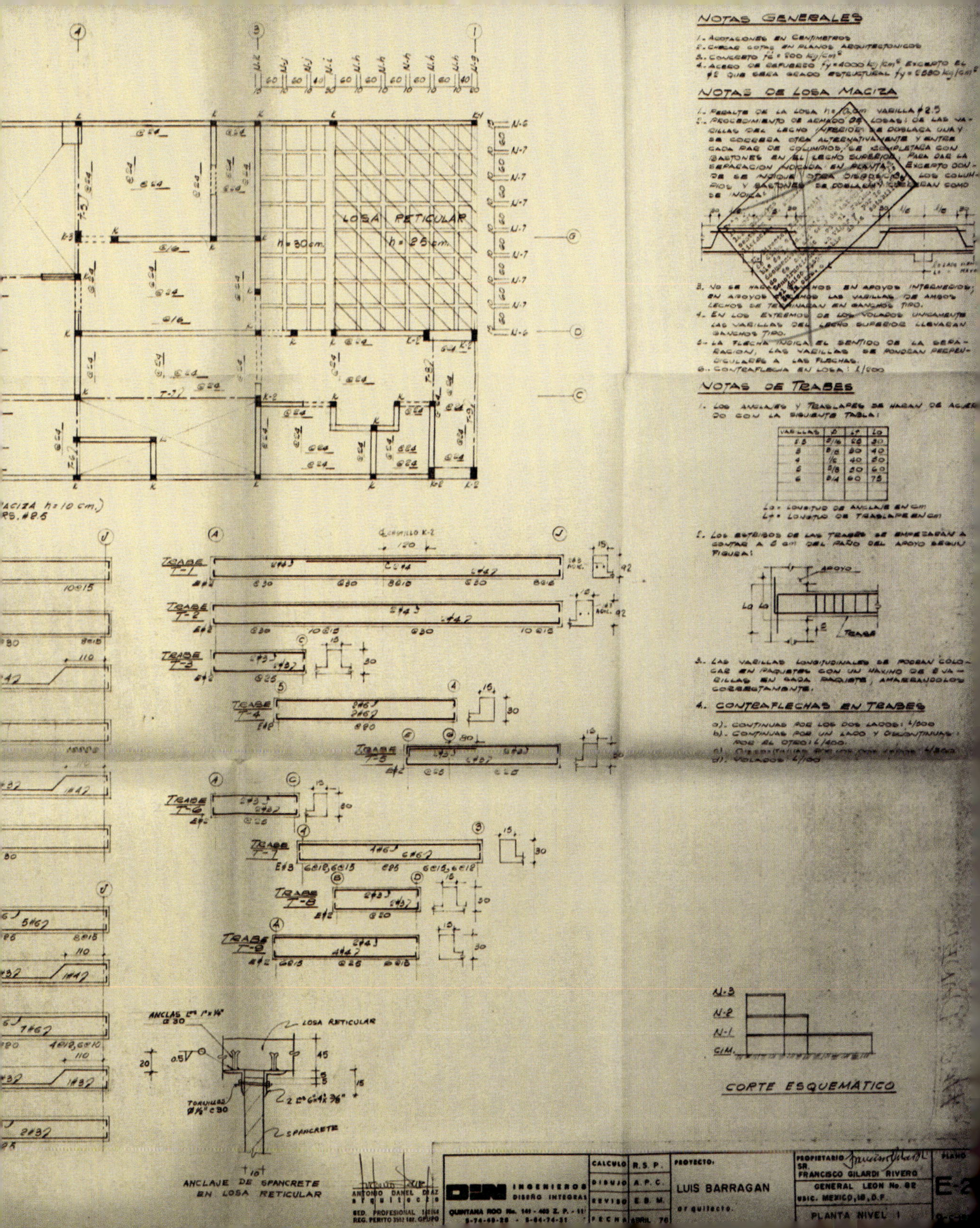
NOTAS GENERALES
1.- ACOTACIONES EN CENTIMETROS
3.- CONCRETO f'c = 200 kg/cm²
NOTAS DE LOSA MACIZA
1.- PERALTE DE LA LOSA h=10 cm VARILLA #2.5
4.- EN LOS EXTREMOS DE LOS VOLADOS UNICAMENTE LAS VARILLAS DEL LECHO SUPERIOR LLEVARAN GANCHOS TIPO.
5.- LA FLECHA INDICA EL SENTIDO DE LA SEPARACION, LAS VARILLAS SE PONDRAN PERPENDICULARES A LAS FLECHAS.
6.- CONTRAFLECHA EN LOSA: L/500
NOTAS DE TRABES
1. LOS ANCLAJES Y TRASLAPES SE HARAN DE ACUERDO CON LA SIGUIENTE TABLA:
VARILLAS
Lo = LONGITUD DE ANCLAJE EN CM
Lt = LONGITUD DE TRASLAPE EN CM
APOYO
TRABE
4. CONTRAFLECHAS EN TRABES
a). CONTINUAS POR LOS DOS LADOS: L/500
b). CONTINUAS POR UN LADO Y DISCONTINUAS POR EL OTRO: L/400.
d). VOLADOS: L/100
LOSA RETICULAR
h = 30 cm.
h = 25 cm.
Trabe T-1
Trabe T-2
Trabe T-3
Trabe T-4
Trabe T-5
Trabe T-6
Trabe T-7
Trabe T-8
Trabe T-9
LOSA RETICULAR
SPANCRETE
ANCLAJE DE SPANCRETE EN LOSA RETICULAR
N-3
N-2
N-1
CIM.
CORTE ESQUEMATICO
ANTONIO DANIEL DIAZ
arquitecto
INGENIEROS
DISEÑO INTEGRAL
CALCULO R.S.P.
DIBUJO A.P.C.
REVISO E.B.M.
FECHA ABRIL 76
PROYECTO:
LUIS BARRAGAN
arquitecto.
PROPIETARIO
SR.
FRANCISCO GILARDI RIVERO
GENERAL LEON No. 82
UBIC. MEXICO, 18, D.F.
PLANTA NIVEL 1
PLANO
E-2

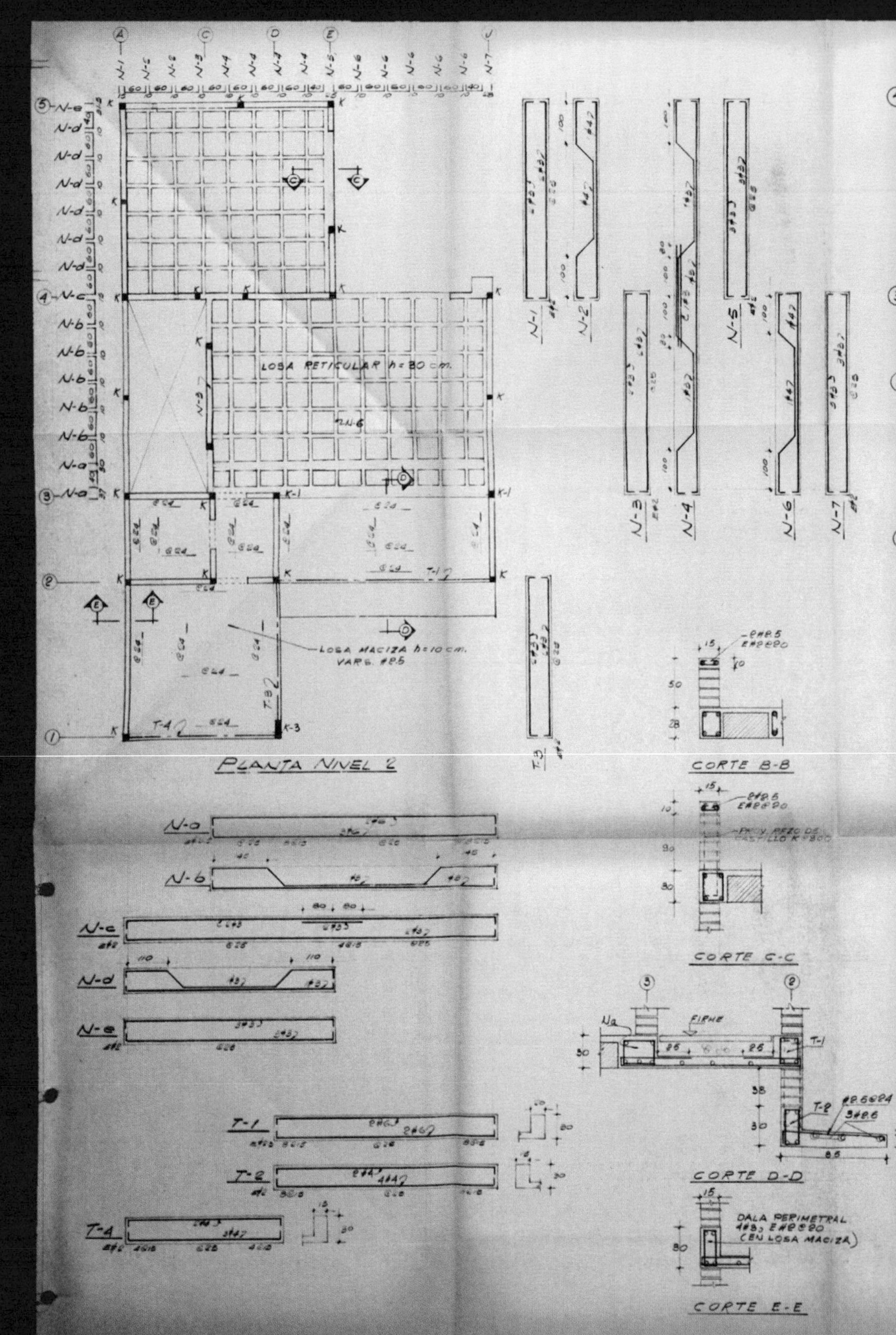

LOSA RETICULAR h=30 cm.
LOSA MACIZA h=10 cm.
VARS. #2.5
PLANTA NIVEL 2
CORTE B-B
CORTE C-C
CORTE D-D
CORTE E-E
DALA PERIMETRAL
(EN LOSA MACIZA)
FIRME

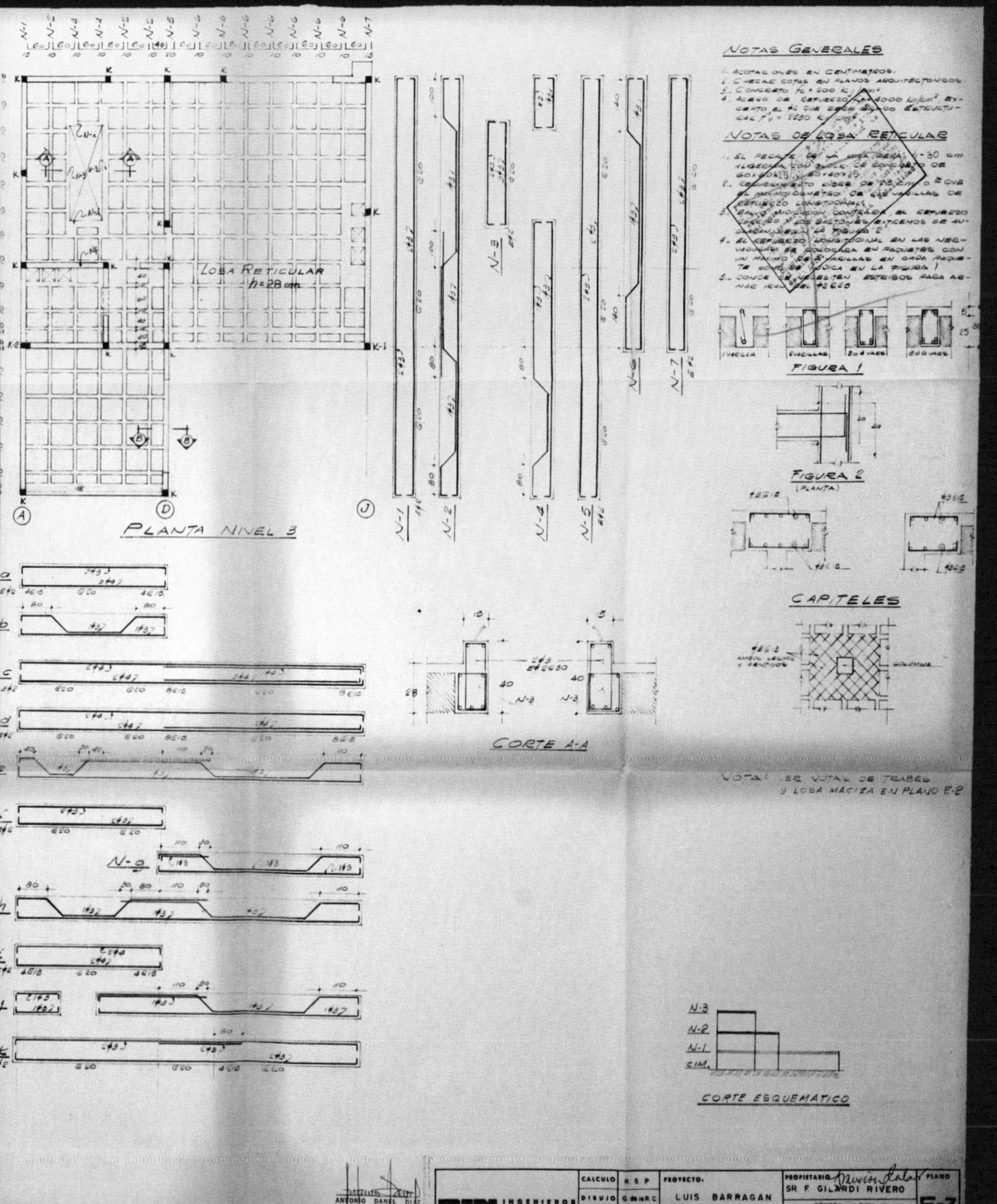

NOTAS GENERALES
NOTAS DE LOSA RETICULAR
LOSA RETICULAR
h=28 cm
PLANTA NIVEL 3
FIGURA 1
FIGURA 2
(PLANTA)
CAPITELES
COLUMNA
CORTE A-A
CORTE ESQUEMATICO
N-3
N-2
N-1
CIM.
Y LOSA MACIZA EN PLANO E-2
ANTONIO DANIEL DIAZ
arquitecto
INGENIEROS
DISEÑO INTEGRAL
CALCULO
R. S. P.
DIBUJO
REVISO
E. B. M.
FECHA
ABRIL 76
PROYECTO.
LUIS BARRAGAN
ARQUITECTO
PROPIETARIO
SR. F. GILARDI RIVERO
GENERAL LEON No 82
MEXICO 18 D.F.
UBIC.
PLANTAS 2o y 3er NIVS.
PLANO
E-3

Log and Testimonials

Junya Ishigami 14/3/2019

Barragán
Música.
Hockney.
caballos.
una casa en
la galaxia.
noviembre 2010

Neri
DEAR MARTIN 10/25/13
HAPPY BIRTHDAY!
LYNDON NERI

BARAGAN + BENSIMON
BB FOR One place!!!

Patrik Schumacher

to Martin

no end …

Tom Kundig

3.11.14

THE PLANE, NOT DECOR
STEPHEN PRINA
LOS ANGELES / CAMBRIDGE 2013

ARCHITEKTUR IST
(DOCH) EIN DING,

W.P.

4
12
15

TO MARTIN: "TRUTH IS THE DAUGHTER OF TIME".... SOPHOKLES

BARRAGAN

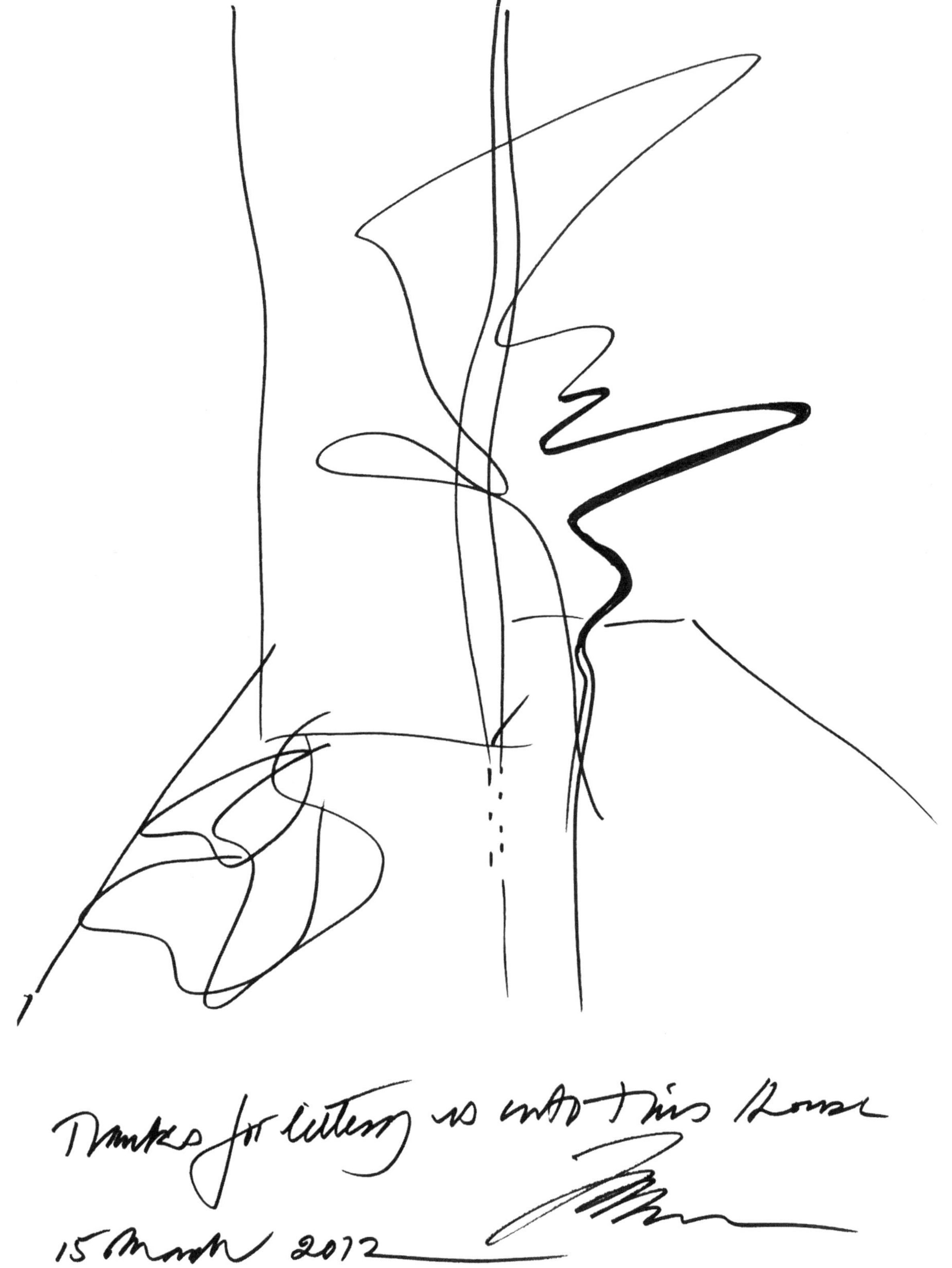
Thanks for letting us into this house
15 March 2012

Casa Gilardi
11/2022

Architecture as Landscape...

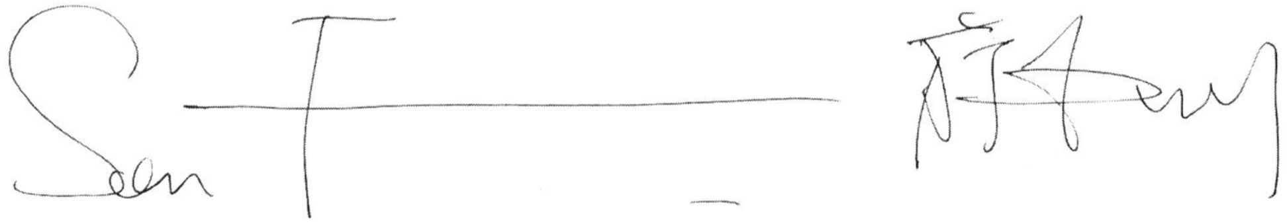

Sou F—— 藤本

2012.03.13

Toyo Ito
05 Oct. 2009

Dearest M.

This is the first sketch of
our infinite dinner table project.

To infinity more dreams.

♥

x

Sumayya.

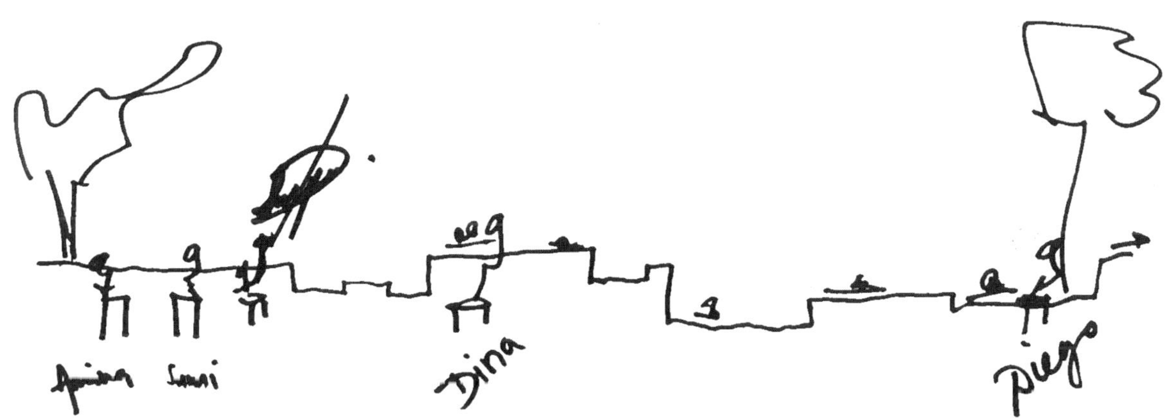

Now, feel free to sketch here!

ヒラルディ邸

伊東豊雄

私がメキシコに強く惹かれるようになったのはプエブラにあるメキシカン・バロックの教会に案内されてからである。
16 世紀にスペイン人が入植した際、彼らは原住民を改宗させるためピラミッドを破壊し、その上に原住民の職人の手によって素朴な教会を建てた。それらは黒いマリア像であったり、可愛らしいエンジェルが宙に飛び交う、プリミティブでありながら生命力に溢れた明るい建築であった。
そうした生命力や明るさは今日のメキシコにも充満している。経済的には決して豊かな国とは言えないが、強い陽光と生活をエンジョイする人々の姿に、私はメキシコを訪れるたびにエネルギーをもらう。
ヒラルディ邸は長方形プランの直線のみによって構成されたモダニズムの建築である。外部も内部も余分な要素をそぎ落とされた抽象的な面の組み合わせでつくられている。素材もほとんどの壁は粗いモルタルの掻き落としで仕上げられている。
しかしこの住宅の内部にはメキシコ独特の生命力が漲っている。強い陽光とそれを受け止める強い色彩、水、それらが重なり合って我々は住宅の内部にいることさえ忘れ、光と色彩によるメキシコの自然の空間に浮かんでいるように感ずるのだ。
その印象はまるで抽象的な絵画の空間の内に身を置いて居るようだ。
この住宅はルイス・バラガン晩年の作だし、バラガン自身寡黙で静かな人だったと言われているが、どこにこの生命力溢れる空間をつくるエネルギーを秘めていたのだろうか。
モダニズムの空間の内に込められた内なるメキシコの自然、それは我々に多くの力と勇気を与えてくれる。

The moment I first felt a strong attraction to Mexico was when I toured a Baroque-style Mexican church in Puebla.

It had been built in the 16th century, after the Spanish had colonized the territory, destroyed the pyramids, and convinced the indigenous people to build this church instead, "the house of God", for the sole purpose of converting them to Christian beliefs. Inside, there were images of an indigenous Virgin Mary surrounded by beautiful angels flying everywhere, and although the architecture was rudimentary, it was also undeniable that light and life danced inside it.

That amazing light and vitality permeates Mexico to this day. Although the country may not be considered a major economic power, the way people enjoy the bright sun and, above all, life has always energized me whenever I have visited.

The Gilardi House was built with straight and uncut lines in a longitudinal approach, which is rooted in modern architecture. All superfluous elements have been eliminated, both outside and inside. Most of the walls have a rustic mortar finish, and there are some very simple materials in the rest of the house.

But the house is full of a particularly Mexican vitality. In addition to intense light and a great mix of colors, it includes a very special element – water – that seems to cleanse the soul, making us forget that we're in a room, giving us the feeling of being enveloped by this Mexican space of light and color.

It creates the impression of being in the middle of an abstract painting.
This house was built in Luis Barragán's later years, by a man who was reputed to be calm and taciturn, which leads us to ask ourselves: Where did he get the energy to create this space that is so full of life?

If one thing is clear, it's that the Mexican nature contained in this modern space gives those of us who contemplate it a strength and courage we didn't know we needed.

Gilardi House

Charles Renfro
Diller Scofidio + Renfro

Interiority suggests a place without access to the outside and can yield a completely self-referential, solipsistic or even narcissistic state of being. Interiority can lead to self- absorption, self-consciousness, boredom, anxiety, suffocation (or masturbation.) Or it can lead to Casa Gilardi, a completely interior work suffused with light, color, pleasure, joy and freedom. For me, the removal of distractions from the outside world (only a tree reminds us of it) and the inside world (there are no light switches, wall sockets, light fixtures, baseboards, reveals, kick plates, edging or thresholds) leads to a sense of abandonment of the everyday and a total engagement with one's own senses. More like a theater set that a body moves through, it is a cinematic gesamptkunstwerk offering a palliative to the over stimulation of our modern life. It also produces an immersive experience more akin to being in a club than a house: Casa Gilardi is more like a drug than a building, transporting residents and visitors into an altered state of being without a hangover.

Neil Denari
NMDA

From the chevron wood garage door on the street to the sun-streaked swimming pool at the back of a famous slice of the Mexico City urban fabric, the Casa Gilardi is a Cartesian Vessel filled with every idea Luis Barragan had, of which, depending on how you look at, there were very few or unthinkably too many. Carried out long after he had stopped active practice[1], it is a kind of second life project that can only be compared to Sigurd Lewerentz's St. Peter's at Klippin[2], both in terms of point in life and in the miraculous compression of ideas, each avoiding calamitous outcomes in their last works. Indeed, late works by many architects are the strangest and often, least compelling, driven by flights of fancy, hubris, lack of self-awareness, or an odd decline in skills. In the case of Casa Gilardi however, Barragan imposed his last built will and testament, his last offering to the architectural gods[3], onto a site with a single Jacaranda tree begging to be preserved. He did not simply spare the tree however, in fact he converted it into his erstwhile client, building around it a house that two bachelors would have to figure out how to inhabit.

That approach, an architect searching for all sentient things in a site, as if trees, water, soil, clouds, and shadows could be thought of as active, feeling participants in a design process, might seem conventional for a phenomenologist as was Barragan, yet my feeling is that the humans involved, here the original clients Pancho Gilardi and Martin Luque, are less the real beings and more the ghostly apparitions that move mysteriously though solid eternal spaces. I visited Casa Gilardi, but unlike most, I did not take a single photograph, preferring to remember it only vaguely[4]. In that sense, I inhabited it naturally, in the state Barragan might have preferred. What engenders that sense of vagueness is at the heart of his work in that it is spatially manifold, possibly even schizophrenic. Part monastic cell structure, part Loosian Raumplan, and part Shinden-zukuri style space, Barragan fashioned environments that on the surface appear simple in arrangement, yet below the level of obvious perception is a visual and temporal experience that cannot be captured cleanly, either through the mind or a camera. And when imagined through the chromatic world of magentas, blues, and yellows, it's as if you move through a painting that had been color separated into CMYK pixels, the original image never to be recovered.

While the Luque family has spoke of it as "just" a house, as a place in which normal life takes place, for anyone else, the house is just as real, but we cannot live it or see it, we can only dream it. Not every dream is a remembered though, lost in an inaccessible repository of imagined experiences. Like the end of Blow -Up[5], maybe I was never there.

1. An architect never retires even if one doesn't build, just as all architects are "young", so long as they are alive.
2. This was Lewerentz's last project finished just past his 80th birthday.
3. I use architectural gods here to cover more ground in the spiritual sense. Barragan the Catholic may have had only one God that he communicated with, but I sense a diffusion of that singularity when thinking about the conceptual crevices in the work, where other demiurges beckon our attention.
4. In all honesty, I did look at a few images online before writing this short piece, but the images did little to recreate firm memories.
5. Blow -Up, Michelangelo Antonioni's 1966 film inspired by Julio Cortazar's short story "Las babas del diablo", end with the photographer Thomas returning to a park in which thought he witnessed a murder. He finds only mimes playing tennis with no rackets or balls. Then they disappear too, leaving him alone as a single ghostly figure himself. The world is material, we are not.

Ryue Nishizawa
SANAA

ルイス・バラガンの建築
私はメキシコに行ってルイス・バラガンの建築を訪ね、魅了された。とくにバラガン自邸をはじめとした、ギラルディ邸や　邸などのメキシコシティ市内にある都市住宅と庭は素晴らしいと思った。もっとも感銘を受けたことは、バラガンは何も特別なものを用いずに、普通の材料だけでもって、きわめて独創的な建築を作っている点だ。構造は、たとえばキャンデラのように冒険的な構造に挑戦しているわけではない。バカルディのミースのように、大ガラスや大理石などの高価で豪華な材料を用いているわけでもない。また、初期のオゴルマンのように、先鋭的なモダニズム建築を追求しているわけでもない。バラガンはそういうことをせずに、普通の壁と床、ドア、窓、レンガ、木という、メキシコシティの街に溢れかえっている当たり前のものだけを使う。バラガンの建築はハカランダの花のように鮮やかな色彩を持ち、その色鮮やかな色彩がバラガン建築の専売特許のように私たち日本人はみんな思っている。しかしメキシコシティに行って誰もが気づくのは、そもそもメキシコシティは色鮮やかなのだ。赤や紫や白の壁が次々に連続し、メキシコの美しい花や木々と混ざり合いながら、街が出来上がっている。バラガンの建築は、色鮮やかな人工の色彩と、豊かな自然の赤や紫が混ざり合ってたいへん美しいが、しかしそれはメキシコシティでは特別なことではなくて、みんながやっていることなのだ。
そういうわけで、ルイス・バラガンの建築について私が思う素晴らしさを思い切り簡単にまとめてしまえば、誰でも使うような材料と構造体でもって、誰もできなかった建築芸術を創造したその独創性であり、またその独創性が、周囲から孤立したそれではなくて、メキシコの自然や歴史そのものであることだ。
西沢立衛

When I traveled to Mexico and viewed the architecture of Luis Barragán, I was captivated. The urban homes and gardens he designed in Mexico City—his own house, Gilardi House, Ortega House—were sublime. I was especially impressed that he created extremely original works using only the most conventional materials, nothing special. He did not experiment with adventurous structures, like Candela; nor did he indulge in luxurious, expensive materials like marble and huge glass panes, as Mies did with the Bacardi office building. And he did not strive to produce radically modernist architecture like O'Gorman in his early years. Instead, Barragán used ordinary walls, floors, doors, windows, bricks, wood—things one would find anywhere in Mexico City. Yet his architecture is as fresh and colorful as the blossoms of the jacaranda tree, and that vividness is a patented attribute of "Barragán architecture" in the minds of Japanese like myself. When people visit Mexico City, however, they realize that the city itself is just that colorful. The neighborhoods are lined with walls of red, purple, and white, festooned with the beautiful flowers and trees of Mexico. Barragán's architecture is similarly enlivened by its blend of brilliant artificial colors and rich natural hues of red and purple. But in Mexico City, there is nothing unique about this blending; it's what everybody does.

To sum up, what enchants me about the architecture of Luis Barragán is his sheer originality in using materials and structures that anyone might use to create architectural art that no one else could create. This originality is what makes his work one with its surroundings, and with the history and natural landscape of Mexico itself.

Michelle Delk is a Partner, and the Director of Landscape Architecture, with Snøhetta in North America living in New York City, NY and in Denver, Colorado. A passionate advocate and designer of the public realm, her work is evocative of a foundational premise to create places that enhance positive relationships between people and environments. She actively supports a variety of landscape advocacy organizations, curatorial projects, and academic institutions.

From New York, I arrive late in the night for my first time in Mexico City. Whisked away from the airport directly to dinner; an open restaurant courtyard amongst trees reaching to the sky, vibrant voices in joyful conversations, welcomed by strangers as though we're old friends.

Energy builds exhilaration into the late hour. We will all share our work at an architecture symposium tomorrow; sleep unheeded... Present in this moment, yet where am I? Conversations in the street. Collectively we depart and journey to another part of the city.

The timestamp on the first photo, 12:51am

Silhouette of a sculptural tree dotted with dark, wispy leaves; branches framed by soft light exuding from rectangular openings in the façade of a dark building; set against a pure monotone gray-blue sky. My arrival.

Welcomed inside by hushed voices, the family is sleeping upstairs. This is someone's home. This is Casa Gilardi, Barragan's last work. No explanation, no discussion, come in, look around, explore... just be.

A slight sense of trespass underscores curiosity and intrigue. Visceral senses of wonder, awe, and quiet joy shaped by vibrant colors of red, blue, yellow; of the play of light and dark from outside in –and inside out; of movement and passage while wandering, touching, seeing, feeling.

Timestamp, 1:20am

Is it shameful to admit how little I understood of Barragan just minutes ago, and how much I feel I know now? Knowledge shaped by experience; feelings formed by memories. 29 minutes have passed, maybe more, camera forgotten to my pocket.

Barragan's Casa Gilardi is justifiably known for its evocative and photogenic pool, which animates the heart of the house through the striking color of walls that pierce into the depths of the water, dematerializing it in the process. It is impossible not to notice that the reflections of the natural light are constantly changing, effected by both time of day and the fluidity of the water. In the context of these dynamic atmospheric effects, the more subtle peculiarities of Gilardi's section are often overlooked. The house intersects two very different section strategies. Accessing the pool involves traversing the length of the site, with only a few steps up at the street and at the threshold of the stair hall. Yet, emerging into the pool room, one's sense is that you have dug into the ground, with light filtering into this almost grotto-like place from the ground above. The golden illumination in the hallway, vertical cuts in the wall, intensifies this sensation of moving horizontally into a thickness.

Furthermore, although the Jacaranda tree marks the original ground of the house, the majority of horizontal exterior surfaces of the house are at the roof level above the pool, accessed by a distinctly un-door like door. In contrast, the central stair spirals vertiginously up three levels, carved from the solid poche of plaster at the base, but transitioning to thinner white stringers in the upper two levels. Wood treads skin this thickness, cantilevering ever so slightly into the central void with no handrail to stop anything's fall. Where one model of section is activated by moving horizontally into a ground, the other spirals up toward the light with few protections from the pull of gravity. It is interesting to note that these two sectional strategies are both marked in the longitudinal section drawing for the building's construction by the same infrastructure: plumbing drain lines. A gently sloping line, just beneath the surface of the exterior courtyard, links to a space adjacent to the surface of the pool, while a stack of domestic plumbing fixtures is connected vertically adjacent to the staircase. For a house whose iconic feature is water, it is perhaps the hidden plumbing infrastructure that marks its distinctive sectional qualities.

Color in Barragán's Work

Kengo Kuma
KKAA

バラガンにとっての色

物体があって、そこにテクスチャーを貼りつけたり、色を貼りつけるという方法が、20世紀の建築界を支配していた。僕はその方法をテクスチャーマッピング建築と呼んでいる。その方法はコンクリートという物質の性質に由来すると、僕は考えている。それぞれのローカルな素材で、建築を作っていた時は、素材自体にテクスチャーや色があったので、その上に何も貼り付ける必要がなかった。しかし、コンクリートは、その上にどんなテクスチャーや色も貼り付けられるという、きわめて融通無碍な自由な素材であったが、逆にいえば、貼り付けなければどうしようもないほどに、無味乾燥のつまらない素材であったということでもあり、この素材が、20世紀という時代の性格を規定したともいえる。

このテクスチャーマッピングとは対照的な方法を、具体的な、ローカルな物質を用いて、追究してきたのが、僕のやり方である。そのヒントを与えてくれた一人が、ルイス・バラガンである。バラガンは色を用いながら、彼にとっての色はコンクリートの表層に貼り付けられた薄い皮膜ではなかった。色は、厚みのある塊であり、その塊の集合体として、建築は構成されているのである。彼の最後の作品であるヒラルディ邸を訪れた時、彼にとって色は表層ではなく、具体的な塊であり、それが塊であるがゆえに、僕らの心につきささって来ることに気が付いた。

特にヒラルディ邸のプールは、彼の方法をわかりやすく僕らに伝えてくれる。それは、プールというよりは、水の塊であり、その塊は明らかに、水の色をした塊として、僕らに迫ってくるのである。このようにして水を取り扱った建築家は、今まで存在しなかったかもしれない。コルビュジエも色を好んで使ったが、バラガンの水の使い方に比べれば、コルビュジエは表層主義者であり、テクスチャーマッピングの人であったように見える。バラガンは、テクスチャーマッピングを超える、新しい時代の扉をあけた一人であった。

８３３字

When an object is created and a texture or color is added or attached to its surface, the result is the method that dominated the world of architecture in the 20th century. That world, to which I belong, is called "texture mapping". This method and its application are only possible thanks to the characteristics of a very specific material: concrete. I know this.

When I build with local materials, there is no need to add anything to them, since they already have their own texture and color. Concrete, on the other hand, which is insipid and boring by itself, turns out to be an extremely flexible material to which any texture or color can be added, enriching it in a remarkable way. Because of those properties, this material ended up defining the character of the 20th century.

In contrast to "texture mapping", my approach to architecture entails using specific local materials and following their shapes. It was Luis Barragán himself who showed us this path. When Barragán used a color, he did not see it as a thin layer attached to the concrete. He understood it and interpreted it as a large volume, and, as a result, his architecture was formed by series of those kinds of volumes. When I visited his final design, the Gilardi House, I could see with my own eyes how he did not consider the colors as something superficial. They were a mass, which, as such, would inevitably enter into our hearts and minds.

The pool at the Gilardi House deserves special mention: looking at it, it seems to tell us, in a simple way, about the path that Barragán traveled. It isn't just a pool, but a volume of water, which is so liquid and crystal clear that it overflows into our interior, soaking us with everything it has absorbed and that now lives within it. It seems to imply that the architect who built it has not died but is as alive as ever.

Le Corbusier also enjoyed using color, but compared to how Barragán uses water, Le Corbusier is shown to be superficial, even though he declared himself an avid user of the "texture mapping" technique. Barragán went far beyond technique, and that is how he opened the door, for all of us, to a new era.

Olot-México, 16 February 2023

Rafael Aranda, Carme Pigem, Ramon Vilalta.
RCR ARQUITECTES

Francisco (Pancho) Gilardi and Martín Luque, Arcelia, Martín, Eduardo and Carlos.

A picture, a series of pictures, a color, a series of colors: we architects are won over by the beauty that emanates from the small documents that come into our hands. But, often, living amid that beauty isn't so easy. When you've bought a piece of art, but you don't want to look at it, you can turn it toward the wall, put it into storage, hide it from sight so you can revisit it again another day, like someone coming back to a favorite song they had grown tired of after hearing it too many times. But what do you do with architecture when it conditions your life, and you're tired of it because you'd like different comforts, different colors, different light? You can't just turn it toward the wall!

If a work of architecture isn't tiresome, it's due to magic on the part of the architect. If we never get tired of it, it's due to magic on the part of the inhabitants. Learning to love it, learning to understand it, learning to live with it. The dedication and abstinence that is sometimes required, or may be required, is compensated by the peace and joy and the light that beauty offers, which changes every day, every hour, every minute – making you fall in love with it all over again at every moment. So, we can hang our clothes out in the breeze and mourn those who are no longer with us – Luis, Pancho and now Martín, the people who built it. And thank the people who have kept it standing and those who will continue that task with respect.

When you have the chance to meet those people, like we did, and to talk with them in Mexico and in Olot, you understand so much and you feel so much humanity. We want the same thing for everyone who visits the house, even without living in it: for them to take notice and make an effort to be aware of all that humanity. Along with the beauty, they deserve as much.

San Francisco, 2023

Thom Faulders
Faulders Studio

I was in town to give a talk at the Polyforum Cultural Siqueiros. Together with other invitees and instigators, we spent a couple of hours hanging out at Barragan's Casa Gilardi and enjoyed the company with one of the building's occupants.

To me, Casa Gilardi is a house that gets in the way. To get in the way is to create interference, to make that which should be easy into something more challenging, to cause a problem. When it works, the act of getting in the way can be a constructive position of defiance, to obstruct in order to open, to take a stand.

One of contemporary architecture's most iconic photos is of Casa Gilardi's main living area: a dining table rests on one side of the room, and the other half the floor area is filled with a giant puddle of water. This means that fifty percent of the space cannot be accessed - liquid gets in the way. This is brilliant! Leave your feet at one end of the room, and use your mind to access the other. Let your brain experience what you (which 'you' are we talking about?) physically cannot enter. Perhaps Barragan was laughing at the predicament: what is meant by utility and purpose, anyway?
Make a chunk of the room inaccessible, and you get something more! From this interior puddle emerges a red vertical wall, purposefully positioned to get in the way of one's visual grasp of the overall pool. At least during my visit, this wall blocks a frontal view of a large black rock sitting silently in the water, so obviously trying to hide like a small animal without making a peep. All of this interference and obstructionism has a deeper purpose - the photos tell the story best of a room filled with hidden things, like radiance and nuance.

Outside in the adjacent courtyard, high walls limit views outward. Is it really a loss that we only get to see the sky, a well-matched blue to the painted interior wall? At the center of this courtyard stands an old Jacaranda tree dropping purple dots all over the swirling Cantera stone pavers. One of the tree's appendages had been lopped off recently with a saw: the branch was about to run into the purple blossom-color side wall that was getting in the way of the tree's natural growth.
But the Jacaranda wins: confined to the ordered geometry of the courtyard, it spews freeform shadows over every Barragan-plastered surface and lacks no control in doing so. Without so much architecture getting in the way of shadows reaching the ground, we'd miss this rather messy, non-static patterning.

Back indoors, there's a solid double swing door that obscures views of the kitchen from within the yellow-hued entry corridor. This door hinders the everyday coming and going by house inhabitants, and if one is not careful, an out-swinging door could smack you in the face. To keep the peace, a very small fist-size cut-out penetrates the door just below eye level. With this small invention a daily obscureness just became more intriguing.

Buildings should try to get in the way more often.
Architecture should be allowed to get in the way more often.

Casa Gilardi:
A Surreal Journey through Architectural Contrasts & Human Values

Alvin Huang
SDA

"Un poema es una puerta que se abre hacia otro mundo."
(A poem is a door that opens into another world.)
Octavio Paz, "The Other Mexico: Critique of the Pyramid"

When one steps through the *umbral* (threshold) of Casa Gilardi, a remarkable sensation washes over oneself—an immediate and radical departure from the dense and chaotic urban fabric of Mexico City. The air shifts and the light filters, carrying with it a sense of tranquility and introspection. It is as if you have entered into another world, an alternate and introverted dimension carefully crafted by the architectural genius of Luis Barragán. Casa Gilardi, with its profound connection to Mexican identity and its ability to evoke emotional experiences, self-introspection, and reflection, stands as a testament to the power of architecture as a transformative force.

While Casa Gilardi stands as a seminal moment in modernism, it simultaneously subverts traditional modernist mantras like Corb's *"a house is a machine for living"* or Mies' *"form follows function"* & *"less is more".* These statements connect modernism with fundamentally Western ideals surrounding industrialism, functionalism, and minimalism. Instead, I find the -ism that one connects to most cogently when navigating the urban sanctuary that Barragán originally designed for Martin Luque and Pancho Gilardi in 1978 is a fundamentally Mexican *–ism*—surrealism. In Mexico, surrealism has a resonance and symbiotic relationship with the country's indigenous traditions, magical realism, and political and social turmoil. The writing of esteemed Mexican poet laureate Octavio Paz incorporated surrealistic elements into his works, blending reality and fantasy, questioning conventional norms, and exploring the subconscious, making his carefully crafted words the perfect pairing to understand visceral sensations one experiences when entering the introverted world of Casa Gilardi.

Barragán's seminal project can indeed be connected to surrealism through various aspects of its design and philosophy. Barragán's architectural approach, like surrealism, creates a poetic atmosphere that blurs the boundaries between reality and imagination. The interplay of light and shadow, the juxtaposition of vibrant colors, and the ethereal quality of the spaces evoke a dreamlike ambiance reminiscent of surrealist paintings. Surrealism often sought to escape the constraints of rationality and traditional norms. Casa Gilardi provides a sanctuary, a refuge from the external chaotic world. Its introverted design creates a sense of seclusion, allowing inhabitants to disconnect from the outside and immerse themselves in a surreal and contemplative realm.

"Los opuestos se completan." (The opposites complete each other.)
Octavio Paz, "The Labyrinth of Solitude"

Once we step into the inner sanctum of Casa Gilardi, we find Barragán's masterful deployment of meticulously choreographed volumetric masses, spatial punctures, and vibrant surfaces. In a manner reminiscent of Caravaggio's chiaroscuro paintings, Barragán skillfully employs an architectural technique that establishes opposing conceptual extremes. The interplay between lightness and darkness, compression and expansion, chromatic saturation and diffusion, and spatial thresholds and gradients gives rise to an architectural experience that gracefully oscillates between these contrasting elements.

Similar to Louis Kahn's concept of served and servant spaces, Barragán ingeniously employs the private areas of the residence, including the kitchen, storage areas, garage, bathrooms, and bedrooms, as occupiable pockets that create spatial pressure. By compressing the entry foyer and central corridor and limiting their exposure to natural light, he intensifies the subsequent sense of spatial expansion and the infusion of natural daylight as one moves into the public spaces of the house, such as the dining room, internal pool (a distinctive feature requested by the owner), courtyard, and sitting room.

Darkness is purposefully employed to accentuate the play of light, while compression is strategically deployed to highlight moments of expansion. The deliberate saturation of select surfaces with vibrant hues allows for the diffusion of chromatic richness onto their neighboring stark white surfaces. It is in the harmonization of these contrasting elements that Barragán's mastery shines through, culminating in a spatial symphony that beckons individuals to navigate through a dynamic range of emotions and sensations.

In Casa Gilardi, Barragán reveals his profound understanding of the interplay between contrasting architectural elements, weaving them together to create an immersive environment that transcends the boundaries of ordinary spatial experiences. Each carefully crafted contrast enhances the other, resulting in a harmonious composition that invites contemplation, introspection, and an exploration of the complexities of human perception and emotional response.

"Las palabras más simples son las más profundas, / las palabras más simples son las más verdaderas." (The simplest words are the deepest, / The simplest words are the truest.)
Octavio Paz, "A Draft of Shadows"

The architectural contrasts meticulously orchestrated in Casa Gilardi elicit an intense, rich, and multi-faceted architectural experience. However, it is important to note that this richness emerges not from an abundance of complex design elements, but rather from a limited palette of simple yet impactful design choices, platonic forms, and a restrained selection of materials. The project serves as a testament to the transformative power of simplicity.

Barragán skillfully harnesses the inherent elegance of elemental forms, the strategic use of color, and the deliberate placement of openings to craft a highly nuanced and thoughtfully curated sequence of spatial events within Casa Gilardi. By embracing the power of simplicity, Barragán creates a space that facilitates profound emotional introspection. Every architectural gesture, no matter how seemingly simple, carries a profound resonance, enveloping visitors in a realm where simplicity serves as a conduit for complex emotions and contemplation.

Within the refined simplicity of Casa Gilardi, each design move carries a significant weight, inviting individuals to engage with the space on a deeply personal level.
The clarity and directness of the architectural language create a sense of clarity and focus, stripping away distractions and allowing the essence of the design to shine through.

It is through this distilled simplicity that Casa Gilardi transcends the realm of mere aesthetics, inviting inhabitants and visitors alike to embark on a journey of self-discovery, heightened awareness, and emotional connection.

"El mundo es un eco de nosotros mismos." (The world is an echo of ourselves)
Octavio Paz, "The Labyrinth of Solitude"

Unlike the transparent modernist icons of Philip Johnson's Glass House and Mies van der Rohe's Farnsworth House, which dissolve the boundaries between indoor and outdoor realms, Casa Gilardi stands as an opaque and introverted world—a sanctuary for self-reflection and profound emotional experiences. This departure from conventional modernist notions underscores Barragán's profound grasp of the human condition and the depth of our innermost selves.

Casa Gilardi, with its secluded courtyards, tranquil water features, and meticulously framed vistas, establishes a profound dialogue between the individual and their surroundings. It emphasizes the inseparable connection between architecture and the human experience, offering a stark contrast to other strands of Western modernist thought that emphasized new technologies and industrial materials such as glass and steel.

In contrast to the modernist ideologies that positioned houses as thrones from which to overlook the surrounding world, Casa Gilardi diverges with intention. Barragán, in his genius, created an internal world—an intimately introspective space where one connects deeply with oneself. Through the deliberate use of a limited and inherently primal material palette consisting of brick and stucco, he orchestrated an environment that fosters introspection, rather than providing a grand stage for outward observation.

By focusing on the creation of an internal realm, Casa Gilardi becomes a sanctuary for personal contemplation, a haven where the individual is encouraged to delve into their own emotions, thoughts, and aspirations. It is in this inner world, sheltered within the walls of Casa Gilardi, that individuals can embark on a journey of self-discovery and connection with their own souls.

Barragán's masterpiece challenges the prevailing modernist mantras that prioritize expansive views and external perspectives. Instead, it champions the power of creating spaces that invite individuals to turn inward, to explore the depths of their own being, and to forge an intimate bond with themselves. Casa Gilardi exemplifies the notion that true architectural brilliance lies not in grandiose exhibitions of power, but in the ability to cultivate an environment that resonates with the human spirit, fostering introspection, and enriching our inner worlds.

"La arquitectura es una cristalización de los valores humanos." (Architecture is a crystallization of human values) Octavio Paz, "The Other Mexico: Critique of the Pyramid"

In reflection, it becomes evident that Barragán's creation embodies the essence of Paz's words. While architecture has historically been defined by technological shifts, stylistic movements, and the political and economic forces, in the end architecture is the interrogation, expression, and ultimately the materialization of our value systems. It is a testament to human values. Casa Gilardi's profound connection to Mexican identity, its play with architectural contrasts, its simplicity in design, and its ability to foster introspection and emotional experiences converge to create a poetic and transformative space. In this synthesis of ideas and aesthetics, Barragán and Paz intertwine, providing us with a deeper understanding of the human condition and the expressive power of architecture. Casa Gilardi invites us to step through its doors, to embark on a journey of self-discovery, and to embrace the intricate relationship between architecture and our own emotions, aspirations, and cultural heritage.

Upon reflection, it becomes apparent that Barragán's creation encapsulates the very essence of Paz's words. Throughout history, architecture has been defined by technological advancements, stylistic movements, and the influence of political and economic forces. However, at its core, architecture is an embodiment of our value systems—a profound testament to human values themselves.

Casa Gilardi stands as a profound expression of Mexican identity, skillfully weaving together architectural contrasts, embracing simplicity in design, and fostering introspection and emotional experiences. It emerges as a poetic and transformative space, a convergence of ideas and aesthetics that intertwines the genius of Barragán and the insightful vision of Paz. Together, they offer us a profound understanding of the intricacies of the human condition and the boundless expressive power of architecture.

In Casa Gilardi, Barragán and Paz offer us a glimpse into a realm where architecture becomes a conduit for the exploration of our values, emotions, and cultural heritage. It is an invitation to embrace the profound and intricate relationship between architecture and the human spirit, and to celebrate the transformative potential that lies within the built environment.

M.Arch, José Luis Alvarez Tinajero
Angelina 19
Álvaro Obregón
CP 01000
Mexico City

Gerard Loozekoot
UNStudio Amsterdam
Stadhouderskade 113
1073 AX Amsterdam
The Netherlands

Venice, 19 May 2023

Intro

In a time dominated by social media, quick communication and short text messages, writing a letter may seem a little strange. However, through the process of writing a personal letter, I can not only share in more depth the experience I had when visiting Le Casa Gilardi with José in April 2014 and the conversations we enjoyed together, but also reflect on what we can learn from Barragan and Le Casa Gilardi in particular, in light of the challenges we face as architects today.

Dear José,

Thank you for inviting me to become part of the book memories, especially because you know that Barragan has played an important role in my professional work as an architect, but also, as a friend, I know how much work it is to deep dive into a project such as this. I, for one, am happy that you decided to dedicate your time to researching and analyzing the background and thoughts behind this project, and that, in so doing, you are publishing material that has been hidden for so long.

I have just returned from the Biennale in Venice, where the Curator Lesly Lokko has created an overwhelming experience; one that provides important reflections on topics that are essential to the challenges architecture is facing in 2023. Environmental, societal, political, social injustice, de-colonization, de-carbonization, water management, energy, economics: all critical topics and challenges that we as human beings are currently facing. But where can we find the answers? Or are we, as architects, going to freeze, sit still and wait? Because whatever we do, it will never be good enough. With my partner Gieneke, while sitting on a terrace in Venice, we were in fact wondering how it was in the time of Barragan, and so I shared with her the stories of the first friendly conversations you and I shared.

While times have changed, Barragan went against the mainstream approach of his time, of functionalism and the outcomes of the CIAM congresses, because he believed that, rather than being a machine to live in, a house should instead be an architecture of emotion. Barragan used raw materials, combining these with a dramatic use of light and color. As an answer to the uncertainties of his times, he created subtle and lyrical atmospheres; he came with poetry. Our conversations drifted in the same direction: Can we face the challenges of these times with art and poetry? Can we, with our work, demonstrate the hope and optimism that we as architects are famous for? But also, can we yet go back to the time before concrete and steel where the dominant construction materials?

Stadhouderskade 113
PO Box 75381
1070 AJ Amsterdam

T +31 (0)20 570 20 40
F +31 (0)20 570 20 41
info@unstudio.com

ING Bank Amsterdam
Account 67.15.29.501
IBAN NL79INGB0671529501

ABN AMRO Bank Amsterdam
Account 41.20.70.510
IBAN NL98ABNA0412070510

BTW (VAT) Number
NL801815551B01
Chamber of Commerce

In the 1990's I was a student in Delft, in the Netherlands. Our educational system was built on the Delftse-school, in the line of the modernists. Everything needed to be explained. In the thinking of the modernists, the line and the plane were key and color was 'not done', unless it was functional. This is when I was first introduced to the work of Barragan, who, in contrast, was not afraid to use color in architecture. His belief in the power of emotional connection finally gave me hope that there were new forms to explore. I have always perceived colors as being connected to numbers and names, and I thought that everybody experienced them in this way. It was only during my study that I realized this was not in fact the case. So as you can perhaps imagine, the modernistic training I received felt slightly hostile to me.

When I later worked on projects with Ben van Berkel and the team at UNStudio, I immediately understood that because Ben had not been educated in Delft, his vision of architecture was fundamentally different. The research that we carried out and the organizational models that we developed at UNStudio were there to support public constructions of interaction. Our intention was to bring the buildings alive and to celebrate esthetics and poetry. The computer was, and still is, the principal tool we use to test and develop our architecture. But we also use computation for research. In the field of color, we have collaborated with paint manufacturers, collected color charts from all over the world and investigated colors from their use is cosmetics to how they appear in light spectrums. To be honest, we still have a lot of fun doing this kind of research.

The first ten years of UNStudio was in fact identified as 'the blue period'. Ben and his team used the color blue in a significant number of their early projects. This was because blues can change color. So throughout the day and over the seasons, the buildings and structures would constantly undergo subtle changes in appearance, giving the impression they were alive and reflecting a constant dynamic of gradual transition. I have also noticed that changes to ambient color in public space can at times be so transformative that it almost feels as though you are experiencing another space.

In my first ten years at UNStudio I worked with Ben and his team on projects such as a laboratory in Groningen (green), two towers in Arnhem (green and blue), a theater in Lelystad (orange), the A2 in Den Bosch (yellow/green), a residential development in Suwon (yellow/green/blue), the Astellas HQ (purple/green), a pavilion in Qingdao (yellow/red), the facade of a tower development in Daegu (orange/yellow/green and blue) and at least a dozen other projects where we could use color as a social driver and cultural connector. And we were challenged with each and every one of them: why did we want to use this color? These challenges came from politicians to real estate specialists, but especially from other architects. We always noticed a real fear in using colors.

adhouderskade 113
) Box 75381
70 AJ Amsterdam

T +31 (0)20 570 20 40
F +31 (0)20 570 20 41
info@unstudio.com

ING Bank Amsterdam
Account 67.15.29.501
IBAN NL79INGB0671529501

ABN AMRO Bank Amsterdam
Account 41.20.70.510
IBAN NL98ABNA0412070510

BTW (VAT) Numbe
NL801815551B01
Chamber of Comm

Then in 2014 you invited me to Mexico for a conference. During the preparations we talked for hours about color and what its meaning is for architecture. It was immediately clear to both of us that we had to visit Barragan projects. I had never traveled to Mexico before and was very curious to see Barragan's work in person. And in you I found the perfect guide.

You certainly didn't disappoint me. It was a wonderful trip with long days and many conversations. So it was also clear that the theme of the lecture should be about the use of color. We were able to use the momentum to talk with students and Mexican architects about the power of color, and that was a great experience.

During the lecture I also shared one of Le Corbusier's famous quotes: " What shimmering silks, what fancy, glittering marbles, what opulent bronzes and golds! .... Let's have done with it ...... It is time to crusade for whitewash."Le Corbusier, 1925, The Decorative Art of Today

The main reason we added this to the presentation was because it showed the difference between the functional approach and the poetic approach, and because Barragan met Le Corbusier during his study trip to France. It's a moment in time where the differences between the answers to the questions of a certain time were clearly expressed. But it also showed that as an architect you have a choice, machine vs emotion. I still find it striking how from a functional perspective everything is brought back to economics, while from an engineering or financial perspective it comes down to functionality.

Preparing the lecture was already a great experience. I then had the unique opportunity to work on quite some projects, across different continents. And I had been able to experiment with the use of color. Sharing this with you and the audience was already proof in itself. Yes, we do need to deal with environmental, political, social and geo-political questions. And we have our principles. But we are also trained as architects who through their work, can show different ways forward.

The last image I showed in the presentation was reflecting upon the growth of the world population from 4 billion in 1970 (when I was born) to 7 billion in 2014. Now, in 2023, the world population has reached around 8 billion and continues to grow. This is of course out of our control. But when Covid-19 hit us in 2019 we realized that everything is relative. And in 2019 we were again trying to organize a lecture in Mexico and a visit to some projects. I can still see the disappointment in your eyes because I didn't know how we could get the insurance arranged to travel abroad. The whole world was suddenly colored orange, while we were only permitted to travel in a green and yellow world. But this was also a wake-up call, because we truly do need to change and time is of the essence. We simply have to find different ways to build our buildings and cities.

Stadhouderskade 113
PO Box 75381
1070 AJ Amsterdam

T +31 (0)20 570 20 40
F +31 (0)20 570 20 41
info@unstudio.com

ING Bank Amsterdam
Account 67.15.29.501
IBAN NL79INGB0671529501

ABN AMRO Bank Amsterdam
Account 41.20.70.510
IBAN NL98ABNA0412070510

BTW (VAT) Number
NL801815551B01
Chamber of Commerce

And even while we don't yet have all the answers and still depend on politics, economical systems and issues that are larger than large, we realize that without change we will destroy what we have.

I suppose that is what has been puzzling me about this year's Venice Biennale. It demonstrates a kind of activism for change and it speaks out to our industry. But it also looks for solutions. It looks for hope. And I think we both know that analyzing Barragan will bring a spark of hope to the next generation.

There are three things that I particularly remember about La Casa Gilardi and that I would like to share with you here. I'm not sure if your findings are the same, or if you see it differently, but as a friend and fellow architect, I'm sure you would appreciate me sharing my perspective. Perhaps I didn't need to write a long letter to do so, but as I mentioned previously, sometimes a longer letter also enables a more personal exchange.

The first thing is the journey through the house that ends at the dining table. In my houseboat in Amsterdam, the dining table is also the place where all the talking happens. That's where we meet our friends and share our stories. When you and I walked around in the space with the dining table, with the blue wall behind us and the red wall in front, we were able to imagine sitting there and sharing stories about our adventures. Functionally it doesn't make complete sense, but as in all good stories of adventures, it is the atmosphere that brings it alive; that creates depth and inspires you to share more.

It encourages the imagination and reflections.The space itself makes that you enjoy being there. It makes you want to return, because it aids in the creation of positive and good memories.

When we were walking through the house, we also discussed Ben van Berkel's teaching at the Staedelschule in Frankfurt. Ben had asked his students why people prefer to live in a holiday home; why is that preferable to their own home? This is a question that has kept our office busy for years and brings me to the second point, because La Casa Gilardi feels like a holiday home. Barragan's poetic approach made this possible. It makes the owners truly love their house and in a way it becomes sustainable only because of this. The soul of the house is what has made it stand out for a century. No economical CAPEX model would be able to calculate the value and no bank would accept this as a basis for a mortgage. But it's the reality, it's undeniable proof.

adhouderskade 113
) Box 75381
70 AJ Amsterdam

T +31 (0)20 570 20 40
F +31 (0)20 570 20 41
info@unstudio.com

ING Bank Amsterdam
Account 67.15.29.501
IBAN NL79INGB0671529501

ABN AMRO Bank Amsterdam
Account 41.20.70.510
IBAN NL98ABNA0412070510

BTW (VAT) Numbe
NL801815551B01
Chamber of Comm

The third and last point is the garden. The pink/purple wall there is in fact similar to the color we used for the exhibition "Holiday Home" at the ICA in Philadelphia in 2006, the atrium in the Agora Theatre in Lelystad in 2007 and the "Motion Matters" exhibition in Cambridge 2011. When you and I were in the garden, we reflected on the use of this color. It's a color that changes through light. Because it contains a touch of blue, it can turn from pink, when there is a lot of light, to purple when there is none. This means that it is very different during the day than in the evening, with the effect that you almost feel as though you are in another space. Our architectural minds went even further, we even thought that perhaps Barragan used this color to psychologically increase the size of the house. Imagine that because of the color change, you could feel as though you have two different gardens. Then you experience your house as being bigger. You actually create an experience of more square meters, simply through the use of color.

Again José, I am honored that you asked me to reflect on Le Casa Gilardi and the work of Barragan. It has brought back good memories of our excursions through Mexico City. Sundays without cars when the streets are occupied by people (it is possible), the green vegetable gardens in the neighborhoods (urban farming) and the villas of Barragan that have stood for more than a century and that people treasure (sustainability). I strongly believe that your book can help to contribute to a future vision by allowing us to learn from the past.

You mentioned that the book will be launched in Venice. The letter you are reading now was written in Venice. And I believe your research into Le casa Gilardi will be a great contribution from Mexico to the theme of the current Biennale in Venice.

I hope to see you soon,

warm regards,

Gerard

Stadhouderskade 113
PO Box 75381
1070 AJ Amsterdam

T +31 (0)20 570 20 40
F +31 (0)20 570 20 41
info@unstudio.com

ING Bank Amsterdam
Account 67.15.29.501
IBAN NL79INGB0671529501

ABN AMRO Bank Amsterdam
Account 41.20.70.510
IBAN NL98ABNA0412070510

BTW (VAT) Number
NL801815551B01
Chamber of Commerce

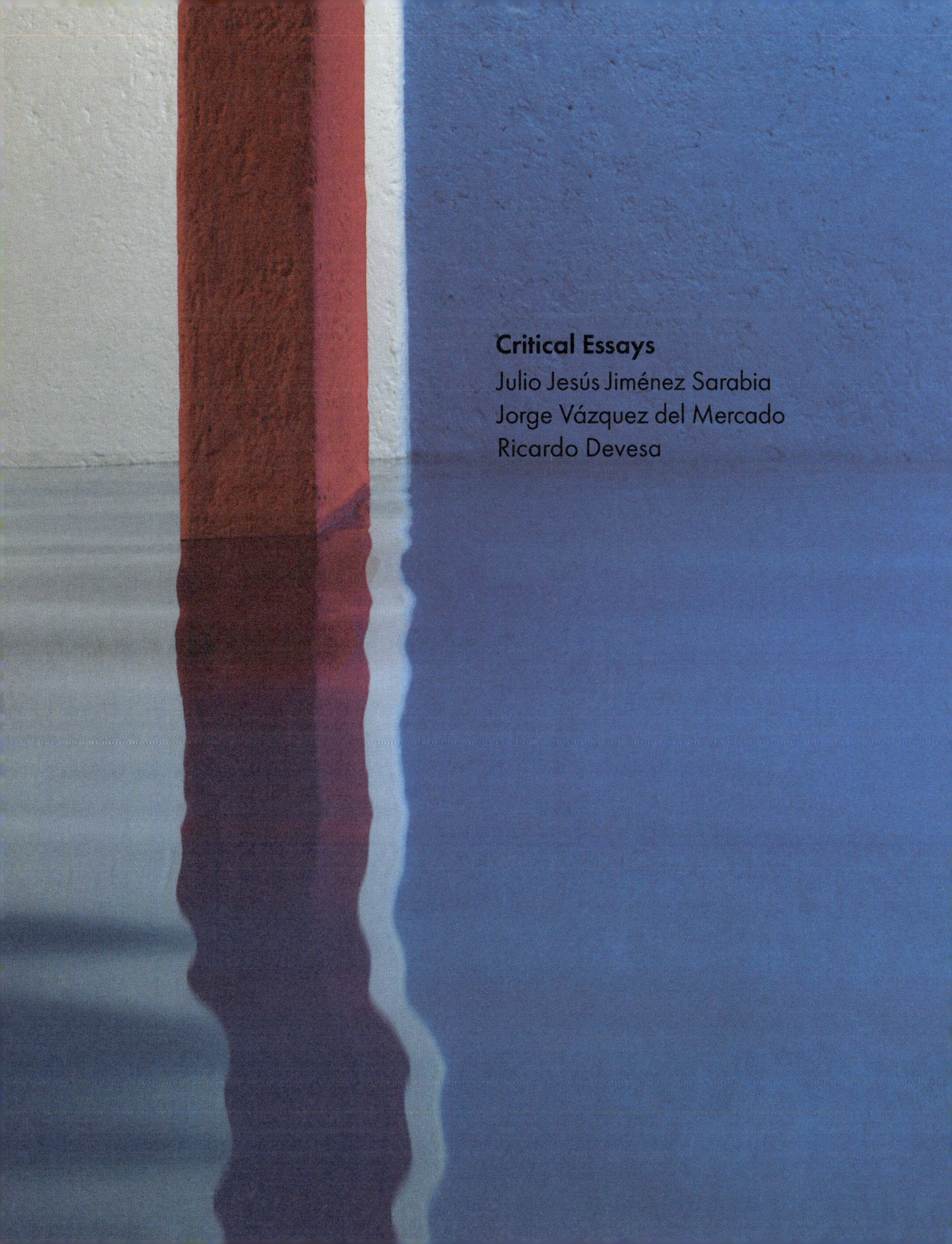

Critical Essays

Julio Jesús Jiménez Sarabia
Jorge Vázquez del Mercado
Ricardo Devesa

Views on Time from Architectural Space: Seven Lessons from Luis Barragán for the Architecture to Come

Dr. Julio Jesús Jiménez Sarabia

We propose seven perspectives that traverse the poetics of Barragan's architectural language in its investigation of architectural space. We posit seven views that, as they are interwoven, culminate in the masterpiece of the Giraldi House, and which, as a starting point and source of ideas for a new reflection, aim to renew the debate on the ongoing rediscovery of one of the greatest architects of our time.

The Pictorial Gaze: Turning Color into Light

This first perspective focuses on the unity of Barragán's thinking with respect to the act of looking. His reflections on living spaces led him to rethink his design strategy through the eyes that pictorial art grants to our senses. Rather than thinking like an architect trained in the phenomenon of composition, Barragán appropriates the pictorial arts to energize and resituate the architectural thought of modern spatiality; in other words, a thought with its origins in cubism that exhausted the purely retinal reflection of Einsteinian space-time. To achieve this, our architect transfers the specific pictorial phenomenology in order to capture, as only it can, the present within the temporal instant through a coloristic sensation, thus freeing our physical body from the architectural object and, of course, from the eye as one of our fixed organs. Barragán's spaces reveal these strategies through their constructed temporality. As the French philosopher Gilles Deleuze rightly tells us, painting reveals presence; in other words, it shows us the reality of a body through lines and colors, to free us from the objective gaze of the act of looking, while, through those same lines and colors, it outlines a reality that is constructed for the purpose of being discovered, as it could never appear in the physical world.

We know that Barragán's extensive knowledge of the history of painting, as evidenced by the books in his library, meant that he had gone down the paths of cubism, metaphysical realism, muralism, surrealism and our deep historical heritage with regard to color. From Picasso to Giorgio de Chirico, from José Clemente Orozco to Salvador Dalí, and from Dalí to Chucho Reyes or David Hockey, respectively, Barragán experiences new horizons through their contributions that let him offer unprecedented proposals within the perspective of the architectural phenomenon. Barragán's aim is to convert color into light; in other words, to paint the architectural space with new sensations and to create new perceptions on the basis of gold, pink, blue and green, where white isn't just white; rather, as it takes on a new coloristic effect, it projects a constructed spatiality through the effects that are generated. In that sense, the Giraldi house can be understood as a colorist whole. In fact, it is a grand pictorial experiment, in which our Mexican architect, using yellow oil paint on glass, like in the Pórtico style of Chucho Reyes, modulates and amplifies a spatial expansion that was perfected in the sacred spaces from the Viceroyalty period, and which takes on a radical relevance here. Moreover, Barragán is a reader of the architectural past, a traveler who seeks out cultural experiences that were foundational for Ibero-American culture in sources from Islam, the Middle Ages or Morocco.

As a creator of novelty within tradition, his intuitions led him to investigate how even water can hold up to light in its material density and how that effect can be transferred onto an architectural space. In the house in question, the refraction of daylight coming from above onto the ceiling or the artificial light at night coming from beneath the pool changes our habitual perception of the material weight of the walls' tectonics, transforming the box-space into light – an Einsteinian equation that transcribes the built spatial environment into an enveloping atmosphere.

Looking toward the Past: Recalling Spatial Heritage

With the Giraldi House, our Mexican architect summarizes contributions from different periods within the arc of architectural history: spaces from the period of the Viceroyalty, the modern period, and the pre-Hispanic period all come into play. In this masterpiece of Mexican culture, Barragán manages, in his assemblage, to both explore and articulate three sensory experiences from our most remote tradition. His profound reading of architectural language revisits three moments from our tradition, which are combined in an unprecedented way – three linguistic horizons from our architectural past, which, together, acquire a new meaning in his poetics. The first of them is undoubtedly the space of the Viceroyalty, which takes on a new form in the entrance to the house and leads us toward the pool, only on the condition of reliving the experience of the itinerant rhythm of the columns from the arcades of church cloisters, but now based on a new geometry that can transform the radiant yellow of Baroque churches into new emotions. This entrance to the dining room-pool is actually not a place, but an act of relating, which, through the phenomenalization of light, deploys a reinterpretation of 17th- and 18th-century architecture, but now with a new, contemporary density of light that paints the architectural space in an unusual way, like a Baroque painter would.

On the other hand, at the end of the corridor, when we open the door, we are transported into modern spatiality. Unlike the previous reading, it offers a synthesis of Dutch neoplasticism and 20th-century German expressionism, but only on the condition of proposing a poetics of water that is capable of evoking the levity of the present moment through its form. Ultimately, the space here is modern, in that it is contained within a conception of the box, as we said before, without walls or partitions, but only outlined by its membrane of light, and self-contained thanks to the red column that marks its limits, like in an abstract painting. In his composition, our painter-architect introduces light and water into the space in such a way that they seem to stop time and reveal their presence, capturing the exterior within the interior in a fraction of a second. The precision of the near-Egyptian beam of light that he introduces into the pool as the sun goes by during the day, and which takes the blue of the landscape as its background, artificializes the naturalness of the blue sky and naturalizes the artificiality of the built internal space, introducing a line of flight as the essence of the exterior within the interior of the house.

Barragán's poetics incorporate elements of the earth: water, light and the landscape, both natural and built, to condemn the prevailing logic of real estate speculation in architecture that pursues closed spaces and that is a bad practice in our cities. It forces us to build today's living spaces in closed boxes between party walls, without hardly any outdoor space and with a suffocating rigidity, as we saw with the lockdown in response to the COVID-19 pandemic.

Barragán takes on an astonishing relevance here, since, with his legacy, he opens new possibilities for architects of the future, who want to reclaim the potential of water, light and landscape in a new way that seeks to destabilize the closed and confined spaces passed on to us from the modern movement, whose principles were betrayed by mass-produced, industrial and mechanized housing in the deviations of the construction industry.

This finally leads us to the third type of space that Barragán evokes, and which appears as the recovery of the stone plaza from the pre-Hispanic period and from 16th-century convents in his open-air spaces. Here, he brings ancient Mexico back to life in the stone surface installed next to the jacaranda tree that gave meaning to the design and which becomes its focus, revealing the passage of time in its continuous metamorphoses, like when its rough surfaces are painted purple by certain natural cycles. Barragán recalls the design strategy that he shared with his friend Louis Kahn years before, for the laboratories in La Jolla, California, advising the American master to build a stone plaza for looking up at the sky.

In the Giraldi House there are no remnants of the city in its artificial exteriority; all that is left are relationships between intimate spaces, in which solitude, magic and mystery shape the passage of intimate and personal time, but elevated to a shared social level. Woven into an endless continuum, these three stages of architectural language, these three kinds of spaces facing extinction, remind us of three moments from architecture in Mexico which, almost like a catalog or an inventory, turn this house into a masterpiece.

Looking toward the Future: The Power of the Image as a Design Tool

For Barragán, the image functions as a design device: that is, as a design tool which, by overlapping visual references, triggers new possibilities for the design process.

Barragán reconstructs the modern design process implicit in work by architects like Le Corbusier and Mies Van Der Rohe, in which form as composition is everything in the creative process. Barragán combines the instrumentalization of the image as a tool to define a mental image with the pictorial investigations of Francis Bacon, who, instead of following the path of cubism forged by Picasso, where the forms of composition are merely retinal, explores other possibilities: in which a photograph, a film, or a book on science or art can unleash new dynamics to articulate a speculative thought process and form a diagram for the creative process.

For Barragán, as for Bacon, the instrumentalization of visual devices triggers new possibilities for thinking about space: first architectural, then pictorial, in the age of mechanical reproduction. Both artists coincide in the strategies suited to destabilizing the mental images that construct our reality.

In this sense, Barragán takes a new path that allows him to break through the murky impasse of the surrealist unconscious as it was explored, for example, by Juan O'Gorman. The architectures of modernity that had pictorial origins, thanks to the legacy of prominent artists like Picasso or Kandinsky, did not exhaust the possibilities of Barragán's explorations. It is safe to say that Barragán takes possession of the image from other logics, from other pictorial perspectives, from other arts even – not just the visual arts but literature and photography – to dynamize and resituate how space is constructed in the architectural practice of his historical moment. Barragán aims to generate unprecedented images and spaces that are different from the paths opened up by the modern movement. That is why we consider Barragán to be one of the first postmodern architects – in other words, those who are capable of thinking about the image as a design mechanism.

Introducing a series of new resources from the landscape, horses, colors and nature implies destabilizing the ideal of the machine. The automobile, the airplane and Le Corbusier's machine à habiter are suspicious generators of modern architectural forms. Truth be told, Barragán is more of a painter than an architect; proof of this can be found in the three-dimensional easel in his house and studio and is embodied in the lectern as a mechanism for the construction of the speculative image. A true laboratory of the image, in which, with its different faces and its rotation, allows the architect from Guadalajara to rethink culture from new perspectives. With this Baroque artifact, which was used as a support for sheet music in churches, Barragán maps the construction of a visual universe in accordance with our contemporary world.

The lectern is actually a hypertextual machine that lets him engage in a critical reading of the construction of discourse in the machine age. It is also important to analyze Barragán's relationship with reading, through books. Thanks to contributions of Alfonso Alfaro we know that he was an assiduous reader of Marcel Proust, researching his literary references and reporting on his notes, and his books reveal him as a reader of the world in continuous debate, taking a critical view and a striking off on a path of his own.

This act of straddling the line between the pictorial and literary worlds makes Barragán a unique artist. His broad and vast cultural knowledge, and his experience of the built world through his interior and exterior travels, allowed him to continually measure himself against giants in different, varied fields. Heidegger, Proust and Pellicer are all included among his readings. The aim is not only an alignment with these authors, but an engagement in a continuous debate, an ouster, if you will, almost a mental exercise that is a preparation for continually standing up to the breakdown of the modern world.

Between modernity and postmodernity, Barragán is a builder of images, which attempt to grasp or hold together the earthquake that the German philosopher Walter Benjamin predicted with his reflection on mechanical reproduction. Revisiting Barragán from our contemporary perspective, from the saturation of images that characterizes our current iconopolis, has the potential to reconstruct a new way of living, an architecture of the future, in which the poetics of serenity, magic, solitude are devices that serve to uninstall and therapeutically cure the problematic of contemporary man.

Deconstruction of the Gaze: Barragán and the Avant-garde

Barragán is the best reader of the 20th-century architectural avant-gardes that developed between 1917 and 1927. Futurism, cubism, expressionism, neoplasticism and constructivism open all the possible horizons of design strategies for modern architects. Barragán takes a design strategy from each of these avant-garde movements to help support the unity of his thought. From futurism, for example, he takes the spatial vision of movement, like when, in the Satellite Towers, the edges that face us have a staggered movement, by means of which the edges of each volume ensure that the ensemble forces us to keep a static point of view, phenomenologically speaking. But if we look carefully, Barragán is also a cubist, a purist or a modernist, if you will, like when he plays with the volumes in the light in the pictorial Corbusian manner, but only at the cost of making each tower a different color. Barragán is the architect who best knew how to inhabit the avant-gardes, adopting each of their contributions as his own.

Within this broad revisiting of the avant-garde, we also highlight the contributions of constructivism, in the moment where he turns the set of towers for Ciudad Satélite into a sign to outline a territorial area, like the Russian constructivist architects did in relation to the surroundings of their colossal, monumental buildings. However, it is no doubt in revisiting neoplasticism and expressionism where his poetic approach takes on the most relevance. We might say that Barragán is a neoplasticist when launches his drawings in plan at different speeds to accelerate the architectural space as we move through them.

And he is also an expressionist at the moment when he appropriates the weight of matter, turning planes into three-dimensional volumes. Here, his poetics take on greater relevance, polarizing these two strategies into a single architectural event, like when he takes us from two to three dimensions at once.

Although it was Mathías Göeritz, with the construction of the El Eco Experimental Museum, who first introduced new strategies combining art and architecture, making the space revolve around the snake sculpture, it wasn't until Barragán built the Giraldi House that a spatial volume was turned into light, in the moment where water as a phenomenological body was transformed into something weightless. Barragán is not only a sculptor or an architect of forms, but a phenomenologist of perception who builds matter from light. He brings in nature and holds it fast through an artificial composition, subjecting it to the control of things that are artificial and man-made, while, at the same time, he plays with the freedom of his gardens, turning nature into culture. Specifically in the Giraldi House, the jacaranda that presides over the dirt courtyard is given a window onto the sky, reminding us of his conversation with Louis Kahn for the La Jolla laboratories. Only Barragán could recommend a stone plaza to the North American master; only a Mexican architect could update the heritage of pre-Hispanic architecture.

Barragán's architecture anticipates the research of plastic artists who build using the landscape and nature. In that sense, James Turell also explored the relationships between color and light, in such a way that, by inverting central vision and peripheral vision, he dislocates our habitual perception of what is natural and what is constructed. And if we look at the Giraldi House from today's perspective, we see how Barragán was already condemning the loss of landscape, light and nature in our cities. Thus, Barragán manages to round out his aesthetic pursuit, introducing into the closed spaces of the typical houses of cosmopolitan cities an outdoors in the indoors that takes shape in bodies of water, color and light.

Looking at the Present: Time as an Experience of Memory

The concept of time that our Mexican architect conceives in his spatial poetics comes from a careful reading of the French writer Marcel Proust, who picks up the concept of time as duration thanks to the lessons of his teacher, the philosopher Henry Bergson, who introduced the method of intuition. And although the philosopher considers time as duration, it is Barragán and Proust who embody memory by using architectural or literary forms. Both start with an archaic time, which as a mental image manifests a deeper experience than what was outlined by the dead end of the Freudian unconscious. In the case of Barragán, for example, his building evokes an architectural ruin through its incompleteness, whether pre-Hispanic Maya or Nahua, monastic or post-Cortés, like the old Mexican haciendas on the ranches around Mazamitla.

What persists are not sculptural forms, but the experience of them as a mental image that remains indestructible and timeless, because it has a more original history – i.e., an archetypal one. In the poetics of our native of Guadalajara there is an architectural past that is the product of a mythical time, prior to known time. True, he is not a visual artist following in the footsteps of Le Corbusier; our alchemist is not interested in physical forms and their play in light like the Swiss-French master, who assumes Picasso's cubist device, but rather the archetypal images that live in our memory, because they are a part of our aesthetic experience. In that sense, the tower, the water mirror, the wall that becomes a floating aqueduct, or a dislocated nature all appear to us not in their linear continuity as a chronology, but as a kairological event, as an experience we can internalize.

In Barragán's work, there is a fight between chronos and kairos. Our experimental psychologist of perception knows that we are time. In this sense, the aim is to make visible what we perceive as reality; that is, to capture the built world through our sensory configuration, to recall it, if you will – not through our unconscious, of course, but through the roaming eyes nestled in our bodies. Thus, our architect of perception deploys the shadow of the cross on the altar in the Capuchin Convent Chapel, transferring its movement onto the wall that tops the golden altarpiece. Or he relies on the opposite strategy, like when he turns the edges of the water in the Giraldi House's vertical, amphibious red column into an optical and corporeal phenomenon, as opposed to a tactile and sensory one, evoking, through a spatial gesture, the immersive experience of Dutch neoplasticism, using light in a such a way that the space yields to the stillness and density of the body of water.

For our poet, the mirror spheres set in the corners sum up the empty space like a revolving circuit. These compositional strategies are evidence that, for our painter of space, it is not the plastic image that matters, but rather the mental image experienced and constructed in a real way, which is even truer than the perceptual image since it embodies memory in its architectural remembrance such that time is trapped in the moment of the event. Barragán becomes the best translator of Marcel Proust in the architectural sphere: his mythical and legendary forms take the experience of the present moment as a point of inflection, and, of course, the memory of the moment that is projected in the image of the future as our mental image tries to grasp a likeness of the constructed reality.

Looking at Oneself from the Body of Water

It would be necessary to inventory all the ways in which water takes form in Barragán's work. A quick review shows us that, for the Mexican architect, water is to be experienced: turbulent and in thin layers, continuous or still, heavy or weightless, opaque or transparent. Notable in this sense is the unbuilt proposal for the water mirror in the Satellite Towers as a site of asymmetry and dissonance.

Looking carefully at the pool of the Giraldi House, what matters is not the space within the architectural phenomenon, but time constructed as an instant, as a present event in our being-in-the-world. The ray of light that cuts through the water is no longer the intelligent play of volumes but the destruction of the box-space, turning mass into energy – in other words, a phenomenal perception that transforms matter into speed. Here the corners are injured by the depth of the color; the ray of light embodies the unlimited fertility of every present, of every moment. Here, there is no idea of time as a succession of hours because each event is unique and unrepeatable. From one day to the next, the house changes continually depending on the time of day, the seasons of the year and the emotional state of the inhabitants. It is never the same. No doubt, the Giraldi House is no longer the Corbusian machine for living in, or Mies Van Der Rohe's standardized machine, or Walter Gropius's accredited factory, but a temporal volume that makes each moment its own. The experience of the inhabitants in their home.

In the corner of this liquid space, our artist opens a weightless dimension of temporal promises. An opening that can no longer be closed because it swings between two poles that accompany the occurrence of the phenomenon.

The first of them is the dimensionalization of light and the second is converting the body of water into light, as opposed to under the light. This coexistence of asymmetrical parts gives us a momentary image of the temporal identity that is revealed to us through artistic signs. In other words, Barragán gives us: a tree for all flora, a wall for all architecture, and a horse for all fauna. A builder of archetypal images, the greatness of his genius is time as space, horizon as possibility. Not series of things, but the being itself of each thing.

The changing and multiple flow of water is, for Barragán, a sensory experience, an integrated totality, a mental image. Because water, for our creator of liquid experiences, functioned as an investigation, as a guiding thread for new sensations, as a pretext for creating new perceptions. The amalgam of the unity of his thinking. Whether it is light, nature or enclosures, water is a destroyer of firmitas. Its system of spaces constructs a bodily consciousness. Thus, the pool is not just a decorative image; it is a being submersed and, in a certain sense, it is a partial object, a bodiless organ that maintains the practical field it possessed before the mutilation. Barragán mutilates the ruins and convents of the haciendas because his starting point is not distance as a geometric reasoning, but rather a perceptive experience of space that has had a prior life and a prior space in the events of the rhetorical architectural history of winners and losers.

The unity of Barragán's thought is rooted in his spatial language, in his philological revision that settled between pre-Hispanic art and the modern movement, between Viceroyalty architecture and geoaesthetic architecture, between Neoplasticism and Expressionism. He manages to rid himself of the devices of the machine age in his design activity. He imagines space in Spanish, that is, with a vocabulary that lets him narrate between the imaginary, the symbolic and the real – between the mental image and the real image.

In the house he designed for the filmmaker Francis Ford Coppola, his aim is to confront the sphere and the plane. The silver of the sphere it is meant to propose a three-dimensional reading that merges the landscape at different times. Barragán is opposed to the representation of geometric space, as outlined by Descartes. His sketches and his speculative images show us that he knows how to convey what it means to be above, in front of, in proximity to, below.

Deconstructing Time with Space: Intersecting Perspectives

The deformation of space in this architecture is coloristic and turns proximity into mere sensation because the color deposits, in each moment, an atmosphere that surrounds the image of a past, whose remembrance of temporal experiences establishes a new awareness of the present as an instant, as a duration that is embodied in the light. This logic of color in space is a new architectural grammar, in which perception slows down, seems to freeze, to come to a stop.

Barragán densifies intangibility, deconstructing space by using time. For our architect, space is real only to the extent to which it has been experienced and remembered. It is fair to say that, like Marcel Proust, he intuits like a mental image in our memory, nested there like a coloring sensation. It is in color that the spatial vectors of our architect converge, so that they can embody certain behaviors in our directionality. The blue of the landscape, as it appears at sunset on the horizon, for example, is studied by our artist of space in such a way that it ends up becoming a smooth and uniform color in its spatial representation; as a result, it can be controlled from a specific diagrammatic representation, cancelling out the depth of the space, as it appears in the Faro del Comercio in Monterrey or the house for the filmmaker Francis Ford Coppola in Napa

Valley, California, where Barragán, in his drawings for the presentation of the project, set the artificial and the natural on the same plane through his use of color.

At this point, it is worth recapitulating: the design intent for this strategy begins when Barragán studies the large model of the Satellite Towers. Precisely in that moment, the native of Guadalajara uses a smooth and uniform blue color for the finishing stages of the landscape, which lends structure, form and contour to the spatial event. The studio photographs of the huge artifact look more like special effects explorations done by a film studio than the work of an architectural office, because the size of the models and the volumetric studies create a clear image that takes the blue of the landscape as its background, in contrast with the compound forms of the towers. A kind of frozen time in the blue of the sky testifies to the evolution of the passage of time in the sunsets. In other words, Barragán uses blue – insofar as it emulates the landscape or breaks up the box – as the finishing touch on a spatial composition. In that sense, we need a new reading of this lesson that is exemplified in the blue wall of the Giraldi House, because in that instance the peripheral view of nature in an interior space creates a built atmosphere.

A kind of framing, like Josef Albers' but three-dimensional, constitutes the places in Barragán's space. The yellow of the sun, the blue of the landscape, the purple of a jacaranda, the transparency of the water – now green, now blue – make up the atmospheric palette of the spaces designed by the Mexican Pritzker winner.

The combinations of nature in light give form to his proposal. This framing of forms provides him with an operating field to capture the passage of time. The paradox is that, without this strategy, we miss out on the perceptual event. Thus, Barragán gives us an x-ray, a snapshot of reality. In this framing, the deconstruction of space operates as a colorist sensation, always contained within a system of walls, lines and plates that shift at different speeds as we move through them.

Barragán frees architecture from figuration as a construction of reality and operates by offering a mental image that is decentered from an outside. As a result, its temporary character is embodied, through the insertion of an interior into the exterior. Barragán succeeds in capturing time in two ways: through the power of the eternal time of the ruin to show the changing passage of time in a colorist sensation; and through the monochrome of smooth structures, which contrast with a variation over time in the reflection of the light that lasts just milliseconds.

Solid colors always appear in his speculative images; they serve as ground and the architectural figure operates, conversely, as form. The coexistence of these two strategies encloses the space. There is no relationship of depth. No uncertainty of lights and shadows. The solid colors are foregrounds, in other words, grounds. The form is the limit shared by both, its outline. His drawings talk of a chronochromatic experience of the landscape, ever changing, which incorporates the passage of time.

The natural space in Francis Ford Coppola's house can be understood like a canvas. Time is no longer in the use of color in the architectural form. The column-planes, now broken up into non-signifying plates, are stripped of a dialogue between forms. In that sense, they break with the narrative character of the volume based on the sphere. The landscape as a solid, uniform color – immobile. In other words, colors in Barragán's work have a structuring and spatializing function behind the architecture.

They are its background, its immaterial structure, which fulfils the function of freezing a moment in time. If the house for Francis Coppola had been built, there would be a coupling between the landscape and the architecture that contrasts and joins together the twilight on different levels of sensations, at first dawn and at sunset, as the refracting sphere of the astronomical observatory would catch a wide variety of captured moments.

In his later work, Barragán disorganizes the forces of nature through walls that become a battlefield. He disorganizes the space of the Renaissance established by Brunelleschi, reversing the Italian's mirror experiment that saw the birth of perspective, now with a jacaranda – a new mirror that is spherical and existential, in other words, panoramic. This gyroscopic vision inhabits the Giraldi House like a champion of modernity and sees as far as the doors of the Baptistery in Florence, silently looking into the future of the Angel of History. Certainly, it gives us eyes of the skin, as Pallasmaa maintains, since it also implies dissolving the body in color, in the movement of axes that are always asymmetrical and that dislocate the body's experience of time.

We owe this to Barragán, because with his poetics he manages to give us a body that only lasts as long as the passing of the light, an instant. This transitory organ now revitalized as a sensation, far removed from the Cartesian perception of Le Corbusier's Modulor, becomes optical and tactile – in other words, it becomes a jacaranda, because surfaces are touched by the gaze. We open a new horizon in the reading of our Guadalajaran architect in resonance with Alberto Ruy Sánchez, who verifies and confirms this becoming-tree with his poetry:

The time of mirrors
is coming and this is how it sets in:
the ground flowering, like the sky,
and the spirit that rises
as the jacaranda flowers fall.
The mirror does not reflect,
it is identical and opaque:
the sky blooms on the ground
and something in us wells up:
a hidden otherness,
a secret, a longing,
the strangeness of loving one another
at a distance or close at hand,
of feeling that in a mirror
of multiplied flowers
we meet without fail,
we gather together and once again
desire blooms.

With Perspective from the Gilardi House: For the Purpose of Enjoyment

Jorge Vázquez del Mercado

On First Impressions

I remember when we organized a breakfast at the Gilardi House for what was then the School of Architecture of the Universidad Anáhuac México Sur in 2008. We invited Toyo Ito, who was in Mexico at the invitation of José Luis Álvarez Tinajero, and I think it was the first time I visited the house, maybe a few days before the event. I had seen it so many times in photographs when I was in architecture school that I'm actually not sure when I visited it for the first time. I entered the architecture program in 1982, two years after Barragán received the Pritzker Prize, so it was a very Barragán-focused moment and postmodernist at the same time. No doubt, there were projects that had been "overexposed", because they had been published in so many places and because we had seen the same photographs so many times. Le Corbusier's Ronchamp, for example: when I saw it in person, I felt like I had already been there, to the point that it didn't elicit as much emotion as I expected (emotion... a term of some relevance in reference to Barragán). The Mies van der Rohe Pavilion in Barcelona was different, Siza's work perhaps even more, and Louis Kahn's, even more, no doubt. For architects, that's part of our job. So, in the case of Barragán's work, and particularly the Gilardi House, it elicits the same "admiration", let's say (a term that I consider an intersection of fascination and emotion) as the photographs did, also recognizing that it's a work with incredibly photogenic elements, regardless of the context in which you see it. The occasion of the breakfast I mentioned above was one where I was dealing with the responsibility for everything going well, but when I was in the house recently just as a visitor (wonderfully received by Eduardo Luque at 9 o'clock in the morning to enjoy the house in the morning light and to settle what I would write for this text), it was different. It's quite curious that the house was designed with a program that accounted for both events/parties/receptions and family living – or, in other words, that it was designed for a family that would have a lot of guests.

In the end, first impressions are individual to each person, which may be irrelevant or of little importance, and the images – photographs or memories provided by visitors, not users – become part of a "Design Market" like Pinterest or some post-truth site (a deliberate distortion of reality), where the work is deemed good or bad depending on its popularity and the comments on social media. From a less virtual perspective, the house does not fall into the category of "masterpiece on paper, nightmare to live in..." (referring to the title of an interesting article by Daniel Díez Martínez published in the newspaper El País on October 18, 2022). As far as we know, everything corroborates that the house was designed for the enjoyment of its owners. This is a commonplace in Barragán's work, the conscious and intentional quality of the paths through it, the famous fourth dimension that alludes to the time it takes to walk through architecture and discover it – especially to discover it. You cross a threshold, and something welcomes you in; then as you keep moving through it, something else surprises you, and, incredibly, that doesn't just happen the first time. That amazement seems infinite; users are constantly surprised in different seasons, at different times of day – in other words, they can enjoy it anytime.

Designed for Enjoyment

If we assume that emotion is universal, we have to recognize that, although there are masterpieces in all the arts, as well as in architecture, emotion is subjective, despite the fact that there may be consensus, again, in the number of likes or, for example, in the specialized criticism that can be accessed in reputable magazines or books – like the one in which this text will be published – or more or less accredited and indexed journals. Some definitions of Barragán's architecture, for example, posit emotion as its fundamental component, specifying that there are various solutions to a single spatial problem. "The function of architecture is to solve a material problem without losing sight of human spiritual needs."

Providing enjoyment for the user, it should be added, alludes to the utilitarian condition of architecture: serving a purpose... We have found, however, that the idea of "utility" can also be imprecise in architecture since a building can be used for other purposes than the ones for which it was designed. A school can become a hostel; what was once a hacienda can be repurposed as a hotel; a bank vault can be turned into a good bar and a space for listening to live music (like El Zinco in Mexico City); even a church can serve as a nightclub to add another example of the imprecision alluded to above. In architecture, not everything, but lots of things, can be used for other purposes, in addition to the ones they were designed for. It is worth recalling that Barragán had a "functionalist" period, perhaps associated with a real estate perspective, but we can assume that, at the time, he was not imagining changes in use in architecture as an attribute of sustainability or the like.

While "enjoyment" is also a subjective term, it can be defined using attributes like calm, comfort, or security, rather than seclusion, mystery, introspection, or "emotion" which, again, is experienced case by case. In the Gilardi House, there is a clear enjoyment that I call, in my own professional practice, "the festival of perspectives", which is derived from the careful composition of each elevation of the house and, especially, a lot of sketches. Visitors aren't analyzing this succession of interior or exterior façades; they're only feeling – perceiving – the effect as enjoyment...the beauty resulting from the process.

Thus, beauty, in terms of what we've described above, is not completely subjective. It is the result of something studied and intentional; it is knowledge, and the viewer receives it in experiencing the enjoyment of the living space. If that happens, it will be Architecture, as Luis Barragán conceives it. From my perspective, again, beauty is contained in the word "livable", referring to any scale, not just that of single-family homes. Architecture's potential (or obligation) to generate beauty, a product of composition that fulfils the need for comfort, security, or calm, is a right that is contained in the word "livability".

The Design Process

A dear friend shared a text with me I hadn't read before. It was called "I work with Luis Barragán" and it was written by Raúl Ferrera (Luis Barragán's collaborator from 1967 and partner in the late 1970s) for the catalog of the Barragán retrospective held at the Museo Rufino Tamayo in 1985. It talks about the working methods used in the studio, in all their projects, and it is very interesting to address the reflection on the design and production of his architecture from this perspective – especially because Ferrara was the one who developed the design for the Gilardi House with Barragán.

Among other things, the text reveals that, after several conversations where they would listen carefully to their clients, they would develop an architectural program, putting themselves in the users' shoes, and immediately they would write a narrative text imagining – "dreaming" – the design, walking through it before they drew a single line; a story of sorts, that is, a literary exercise; something picked up from Ferdinand Bac: "The idea is to 'dream' the project and tell a story about it..." a kind of description of the project as if it already existed. In relation to the Gilardi House, we might imagine it went something like this: There is a wooden door in a small exterior entryway adjacent to the front sidewalk... Then you enter a hallway, relatively narrow, with wooden paneling that hides a series of doors; it offers views of a vestibule with sculptures... where there is a floating staircase on one side. That lets you see another yellow hallway at the back... then we don't know.

Another revelation from the text is color. "Color is a complement to the architecture; it works to amplify or shrink spaces. It is also useful for adding that touch of magic a site needs..." But it was never decided beforehand. They often went to Jesús Reyes Ferreira for advice, towards the end of the construction, "since they recognized he had an almost infallible idea of color and aesthetic taste." Indeed, there can be no doubt about that.

Another good friend was a collaborator of Diego Villaseñor, who knew Barragán very well, and he told me that the story of the dream practice is entirely true. Villaseñor's office was across from Barragán's and the people who worked in both studios were acquainted. Ferrera was very meticulous and Villaseñor no doubt learned that methodology from Barragán, which, unlike a written story, he generally implemented with a pencil in hand on a topographic map of the project site... My friend also told me that what he remembers most about Barragán's studio was the silence in which they worked. Any sound, no matter how minor, was practically shocking. The silence was absolute, and I suppose that's what the atmosphere would have been like when the Gilardi house was built; you can feel an echo of it.

The house presents a blind façade, which Barragán often used in his designs (privacy and gradual discovery... time) and it looks onto the interior courtyard with its famous jacaranda. It is also interesting that, from another perspective on the space, the house is actually two houses, when we pinpoint the living room in a semi-public area, one level above, on the way to the bedrooms, which confuses and dismantles the idea of any functional diagram as a method for designing... houses. During my visit, Eduardo Luque reveled in nostalgia for his childhood home, underscoring the accuracy of the concept "for the purpose of enjoyment", in this case growing up, experiencing childhood, or going through adolescence... And going back to the guests: would they rather be standing? Would chairs be set out? Would there be waiters circulating around the courtyard with the jacaranda that can't be accessed except from the pool?

Transcendence and Culture

"I think the design is interesting, since the plot was quite small. We made the design revolve around a courtyard where there was a very beautiful tree. I think the pool space is well crafted. It is an anti-academic pool; my architecture is anti-academic in general... I think that the colors and light in this house are good, but the courtyard needs a fountain. The fountain couldn't be built due to budget restrictions, and the courtyard was left incomplete; and since the courtyard is the center of the house, what it looks out on, the rest of the house is also incomplete."

I like it. It isn't my favorite by Barragán. It is certainly an essential link within the ensemble of his work, but again that isn't the important thing, not even remembering that, as Barragán himself saw it, the courtyard was incomplete... Why didn't they finish it, then, perhaps some years later? I suppose that, for the owner, the house was absolutely complete, and the architect had exceeded all the client's expectations. Calling it anti-academic architecture is spot on. It would be enough for a teacher to look at the functional diagram of the house, with the distance between the kitchen and the dining room/pool, for it to get a failing grade. Although that is also where you find one of the most emblematic and most often photographed spaces in the history of contemporary Mexican architecture, perhaps a waking dream for such an experienced architect. In that sense, the term "anti-academic architecture" could be translated as "experimental architecture", so unique in the Gilardi House, if we're assuming that there's no place for experimentation in the academic sphere, which is also questionable, or more characteristic of the 1970s.

But throughout this reflection, there is a shadow cast by the elitist and exceptional nature of this type of architecture. When is it possible to experiment? The is the exceptional case of an architecture that few people can afford, but which nevertheless inspired other architectures that could take on a larger, more inclusive, scale – like in the case of the work by Ricardo Legorreta on the Camino Real on Avenida Mariano Escobedo, to cite the initial example... And are these reflections still valid? Does architecture still serve the purpose of enjoyment? Is emotion still a substantial attribute of architecture? Does the methodology of the narrated dream apply to the problems associated with inhabitable spaces for humanity today? How are the avant-garde, speed, the technological revolution, and digital manufacturing related to these perspectives? Barragán put Mexico on the map of the best architecture in the world, with his resounding authenticity that would – eventually – be included among Kenneth Frampton's famous critical regionalism from 1983, but nevertheless, it is a personal architecture that, for many, reinterprets other architectures, and that is designed for the purpose of enjoyment and...the joy of living.

Having finished the text up to this point, I had the opportunity to visit the house again, invited by Casa Gilardi + node to the opening of the photographic exhibition "Sicily" by Giuseppe Leone on the afternoon of November 24, 2022. It was a new experience to visit the house as a museum or gallery, so to speak. It was a very different event format, namely one in which the house was the inexhaustibly photogenic star of the show. It was newly restored, if you can call it that; there was a notable brightness in its colors... and in the characteristic Aguascalientes stones used to pave most of the ground floor. I was lucky enough to talk with Martín Luque, who generously shared with me a lot of information about the house that I didn't know. In the context of this text and from this perspective, it was particularly revealing to me that the house was not only designed for a family that would receive many guests, as we read in the first paragraph of this text. The configuration of the client's family was not even have completely defined at the time the project was commissioned (there was a significant generational gap between the clients and the architect). The building was actually able to function, eventually, both as an advertising agency and as a house, depending on how the young clients' lives developed. In the methodology of the written dream, with all its assumptions, the narrative does not necessarily incorporate the use or the reason why the person is in the house. What you see, what you find, or what surprises you in the dream journey is just being there, regardless of whether you are alone, resting or working. For example: Then you enter a hallway, relatively narrow, with wooden paneling that hides a series of doors; it offers views of a vestibule... - Are there many people around? - with sculptures... where there is a floating staircase on one side. - And employees or people taking pictures? - That lets you see another yellow hallway at the back... - With waiters? -... then we don't know. Nor do we believe in anything except the enjoyment, the joy of living, and the celebration of architecture, which are all evident in the result.

House or garden? Big or small? Blue or pink?

Autor: Ricardo Devesa

The jacaranda, ground floor, first and second floors, cross section of the Gilardi house.

After 10 years of inactivity, Luis Barragán decided to design the Gilardi House (1975-1977), intending to save a dying jacaranda tree in the middle of a plot owned by Francisco Gilardi[1] and Martín Luque. The jacaranda was not just the starting point for the house, it was also the trigger for the distributive and perspective decisions created around it. In fact, Barragán accounted for the morphological characteristics and the physiological specificities of this tree – the intense color of its flowers and its unique scent – in relation to the house[2] he designed.

The pre-existing jacaranda sits about halfway along the length of the plot, a rectangle measuring 10 by 35 meters: specifically, it is located 15.35 meters into the plot with respect to the line of the façade that runs along Francisco León Street and 2.42 meters from the south-facing party wall. Looking back at the design process for the house, compiled by Antonio Ruiz Barbarín[3], we realize that – from the first proposal dated September 30, 1975 – the tree marked the limit of the area occupied by the house, situated along the front section of the lot. In this first version, the program was resolved in the strip that runs from the façade to the boundary defined by the jacaranda. In this proposal, Barragán had already accumulated the entire housing program in a three-story construction, thus leaving the rear part of the plot unoccupied.

However, the architect, responding to the owner's need for a daily swim, added an indoor pool to the back part of the lot. Therefore, the plot was occupied on either end by two volumes, with an empty space between them. The connection between these volumes was resolved through a covered passageway attached to the north-facing party wall. Around the twisted trunk of the jacaranda, Barragán built two walls at right angles to offer it support and protection, corresponding to the façade of the kitchen and the wall that closes off the service courtyard. Accordingly, he outlined an open space limited by those two walls, the façades of the passageway and the pool, and by the party wall located to the south: a courtyard to shelter and protect the dying jacaranda tree.

The program of the house – from the initial phases of the design and until its construction – is therefore divided into two halves, clearly separated by the location of the tree, halfway along the length of the site. That said, the jacaranda does is not related to the front part of the house on the ground floor, nor does it overlap with the square paved area of the rear courtyard. Barragán situates it in a rectangular patch of ground: a tree pit defined by the two walls that protect it, a platform or step, and the edge of the paved section of the courtyard. Thus, the trunk of the jacaranda does not touch the square surface of the courtyard; rather, it becomes the point of a compass, around which the walls, spaces and thus the different rooms in the house, all revolve. As a result of these formal decisions, the tree stands at the center of the house, even though it is not situated in the exact geometric center of the plot.

---

1 This is how the owner explains it: "He wanted to build the house because there was a jacaranda tree, because it was near his own house, and because he wanted to have contact with a younger generation that my friends and I in some way represented." In Enrique X. De Anda Alanis. *Luis Barragán:* Clásico del silencio. Bogotá: Escala, 1989. The Gilardi House was designed jointly by Luis Barragán and Raúl Ferrera.

2 The jacaranda *(Jacaranda mimosifolia)* is a deciduous tree, from the Bignoniaceae family. According to its external morphological characteristics, it is a large tree – 6 to 10 meters tall – with a twisted and irregular trunk and branches, with deciduous foliage and tubular purple-blue flowers.

3 Ruiz Barbarin, Antonio. *Luis Barragán frente al espejo. La otra mirada*. Barcelona: Fundación Caja de Arquitectos, 2008, pp. 264-267.

Hallway, pool seen from the northeast corner, bedroom window and staircase with the exit door to the terrace of the Gilardi house.

Barragán's use of color in the Gilardi House deserves a detailed analysis since it also establishes certain relationships with the jacaranda. White is predominant in the interiors of both parts of the house, although it alternates with strategically located regular surfaces painted in colors. For example, in the front, the door on the first floor, which provides access to the rear terrace, is painted pink on the outside; similarly, the glass of the guest bedroom window, the only opening designed for the façade, also on the first floor, is tinted yellow. The natural light reflected against these colored surfaces invades the nearby spaces and colors the nearby walls. Some surfaces in the back of the house were also strategically painted: the entire hallway in yellow, and a corner wall in the dining room in the same color; the right angle of the pool in blue; and the freestanding wall that rises from the bottom of the pool in red.

Barragán connects the painted surfaces in the interior with a source of natural light. He does this either by using skylights or tinted glass. The color is thus expanded in the space due to the effect of the reflection of the light – and its refraction in the water in the pool. As a result, the interior spaces of the Gilardi House generate changing chromatic effects for the visitor, which come from a few painted and naturally lit surfaces: this creates an intense and variable chromatic atmosphere inside.

On the other hand, through the use of color on the exterior, Barragán highlights the two parts into which the Gilardi house is divided. In fact, the façades of the front volume are all painted pink – except for a corner of the courtyard-terrace on the first floor, which is painted blue. As stated by the owner in an interview, the choice of pink came from him; he told Barragán that he wanted "a pink house", since the color had become a trademark of his style[4]. In contrast, the rear façade was painted white. For this reason, the colors applied to the exterior walls are identified with the two parts that make up the house: they reveal the formal order of its organization in two large volumes intended for two domestic functions: a private section and a more social one – the pool[5].

4 "Entrevista con el Sr. Francisco Gilardi", in Op. cit, De Anda.

5 From the description, we gather that Barragán used his usual color palette for the Gilardi House: pink, purple, cobalt, vermilion and gold. If we include the dark ocher of the pavement and the white, this adds up to a total of seven colors. Three of them are primary colors –blue, red and yellow– and pink and purple are variations of those. The colors considered primary colors are not in their pure state either; they take on nuances from the intensity of the natural light that hits them and from its reflections, as well as from tones that are a variation of pure colors.

Facade and partial images of the backyard of the Gilardi house.

The south-facing party wall, which does not belong to either section of the house but rather to the courtyard associated with the jacaranda tree, was painted a different color than the rest of the surfaces described so far. The client, Francisco Gilardi, says in an interview that "[Barragán] painted the main courtyard orange and white, but he realized that he should paint it the color of the jacaranda flowers and that's what he did."[6] The jacaranda has the particularity that it blooms twice a year, in spring and autumn, and that its clustered, tubular inflorescences are purple-blue – although sometimes they can turn pinkish. These flowers also stay on the tree for a long time, and they maintain their color even after they fall and carpet almost the entire courtyard.

Given these characteristics of the jacaranda flowers, in the following lines I will briefly outline, as if in story form, the spatial changes undergone by the house as a whole – transformations that are due to the chromatic interactions between the house and the tree.

---

6 "Entrevista con el Sr. Francisco Gilardi", en op. Cit, De Anda.

1. A small blue garden in a big pink house. The Gilardi House contains a tiny garden defined by a single tree: the existing jacaranda. A small garden, in proportion to the rest of the house. A blue garden, since the jacaranda flowers are purple-blue. The little blue garden is surrounded by a big pink house. Big because it occupies the entire plot. And pink, because that is the color that covers almost all of its exterior – per the owner's decision, as I noted previously.

2. A big pink house in a small blue courtyard. This big pink house contains a small courtyard. An open space surrounded by the buildings on the site. A square courtyard, as I said, that is blue like the jacaranda flowers; blue from the south-facing party wall; and also blue, although temporarily, when it is carpeted by the fallen flowers from the tree.

3. A small blue courtyard in a large pink garden. In truth, this small, blue courtyard is part of a much larger enclosure: the one defined by the three party walls – rising above the height of the rear volume – and by the pink façade of the main volume; in this enclosure, the tops of the walls reach the maximum height defined by the crown of the jacaranda tree. Consequently, there is a garden that is bigger than the courtyard, which occupies this entire back section of the house. A garden where pink becomes predominant, once again. Pink because it is the color of the façade of the three-story front section; and pink because of the nuances that the jacaranda flowers sometimes take on: a garden, therefore, that is big and pink.

Entrance door and detail of the pool of the Gilardi house.

4. A big pink garden in a small blue house. Finally, this big pink garden can be seen from the entrance to the house, also painted pink, where you can smell the unique scent of the jacaranda when it is in bloom. In fact, from the moment we enter the house, we realize that we are entering a garden: big and pink, because although the interior is white, pink is the color that bathes the interior walls in the stairwell due to the reflection of the light from the pink door sitting ajar on the first floor. Therefore, if entering the house actually means accessing a garden, the true center of the house is what we see at the end of the plot: the covered space of the pool. Two blue walls, intersecting at right angles, bathed in natural light that descends from the skylight and ascends from the bottom of the pool. In truth, this space is the true center of the house. A reflective space, small in relation to the size of the front section. An intimate space, a sacred space. Definitively, this space, small and blue, is the real house, set in a garden that is big and pink.

And so: House or garden? Big or small? Blue or pink? In the Gilardi House, everything is relative. A shift in its character that Luis Barragán himself desired, as reflected in an early declaration: "let the houses be gardens, and let the gardens be houses.[7]" Turning the house into a garden – and the garden into a house – is the result of, and thanks to, the relationships established between the architectural elements and the jacaranda.

7 Luis Barragán. "Apuntes de Nueva York. Ideas sobre jardines", 1931, en Antonio Riggen, edt. *Luis Barragán. Escritos y Conversaciones.* Madrid: El Croquis, 2000, pág. 15.

Bibliography

Alfaro A., Garza Usabiaga, D. and Palomar, J. (2011). *La casa de Luis Barragán: Un valor universal.* Editorial RM; Fundación Bancomer and FATLB.

Alfaro, A. (1996). *Voces de tinta dormida: Itinerarios espirituales de Luis Barragán. Artes de México.*

Ambasz, E. (1980). *The Architecture of Luis Barragán.* New York: The Museum of Modern Art.

Barragán, L. and Ferreira, R. (1985). *Ensayos y apuntes para un bosquejo crítico. Luis Barragán,* Mexico City: Museo Rufino Tamayo.

Barragán, L. and Ferreira, R. (1985). *Luis Barragán Arquitecto.* Mexico City, Museo Rufino Tamayo.

Buendía Júlbez, Juan Palomar and Guillermo Eguiarte (1996). *Luis Barragán 1902-1988,* Mexico City: Reverte ediciones.

de María y Campos, Beatriz and Catalina Corcuera (2015). *Luis Barragán: Arquitecto de la luz y el silencio.* Mexico City: Ediciones Tecolote.

Fundación Barragán (2009). Josef Albers: Homage to the Square. Mexico City: Editorial RM.

Eggener, K. (2001). *Luis Barragán's Gardens of El Pedregal.* New York: Princeton Architectural Press.

Figueroa, A. (2002). *El arte de ver con inocencia: Pláticas de Luis Barragán.* Mexico City: Universidad Autónoma Metropolitana Azcapotzalco.

Fundación de Arquitectura Tapatía (2022). *Reporte al Tapatío.* Mexico City: Arton Art Group.

González, F. (1991). *Ignacio Díaz Morales habla de Luis Barragán: Conversación con Fernando González Gortázar.* Guadalajara: Editorial Universidad de Guadalajara.

González, F. and Zanco, F. (2014). *Las Torres de Ciudad Satélite.* Mexico City: Arquine.

Jiménez, J. (2001). "Luis Barragán: A cien años de su nacimiento (1902-1988)" in *De Diseño. Diseño Arquitectura Arte* No. 37 Año 7. Ciudad de México: Grupo Malabar.

Kassner, L. (2002). *Chucho Reyes.* Mexico City: Editorial RM.

Palomar, J. (2022). *Barragán por Palomar.* Guadalajara: Impronta Casa Editora.

Pauly, D. (2002). *Barragán: Space and Shadow, Walls and Colour.* Basel: Birkhäuser.

Rispa, R. (1996). *Barragán: Obra completa.* Mexico City: Tanais Ediciones.

Ruy Sánchez, A. (2019) "Tiempo de los espejos", in *Dicen las Jacarandas,* Mexico City: Ediciones Era.

Santa Ana Lozada, L. G. (2016). Luis Barragán Morfín: Regionalist Architecture? Academia XXII, 7(14).

Zanco, F. (2001). *Luis Barragán: La revolución callada.* Milan: Skira editore.

Gilardi House
Barragán's Last Witness

Published by
Actar Publishers, New York, Barcelona
www.actar.com

Author and Editor
José Luis Álvarez Tinajero

Editor
Ricardo Devesa, Actar Publishers

Co-author
Martín Luque Pérez

Graphic Design
Sofía Sandoval, Actar Publishers

Contributions
Toyo Ito, Charles Renfro, Neil Denari, Ryue Nishizawa, Michelle Delk, Paul Lewis, Kengo Kuma, Rafael Aranda, Carme Pigem, Ramon Vilalta, Thom Faulders, Alvin Huang, Gerard Loozekoot, Jorge Vázquez del Mercado, Julio Jiménez Sarabia, Ricardo Devesa, César Bejar, Eduardo Luque.

Proofreading and Translations into Spanish
Anna Tetas

Proofreading and Translations into English
Angela Kay Bunning

Proofreading and Translations from Japanese
Alan Gleason

Printing and Binding
Arlequin & Pierrot, Barcelona

Distribution
Actar D, Inc. New York, Barcelona.

New York
440 Park Avenue South, 17th Floor
New York, NY 10016, USA
T +1 2129662207
E salesnewyork@actar-d.com

Barcelona
Roca i Batlle 2-4
08023 Barcelona, Spain
T +34 933 282 183
E eurosales@actar-d.com

Indexing
ISBN: 978-1-63840-037-0
Available in Spanish under the title *Casa Gilardi. El último testigo de Barragán*, ISBN 978-1-63840-038-7

Printed in Europe
Publication date: January, 2024

Sponsors